THE PATHWAY OF NON-DUALITY
Advaitavāda

Raphael
(Āśram Vidyā Order)

THE PATHWAY OF NON-DUALITY

Advaitavāda

An approach to some key-points of Gauḍapāda's Asparśavāda and Śaṃkara's Advaita Vedānta by means of a series of questions answered by an Asparśin

NATARAJ BOOKS
P.O. Box 5076
Springfield, VA 22150
U.S.A.

This Edition Published 1992 in the United States of America by Nataraj Books, P.O. Box 5076, Springfield, VA 22150, in collaboration with Motilal Banarsidass Publishers Pvt. Ltd., 41 UA, Bungalow Road, Delhi-110 007 INDIA

Printed in India by Jainendra Prakash Jain at Shri Jainendra Press, A-45 Naraina Industrial Area, Phase I, New Delhi 110 028.

"The unreal can not have the unreal as its cause, nor can the real be born of the real, nor can the real stem from the unreal nor, finally, the non-real from the real."

Gauḍapāda

"Metaphysical Unity is pure actuation which excludes all passages from potentiality to act; to speak of the eternally present and infinite in terms of even theoretical phases is impossible. Metaphysical realization, rather than a question of actuation-realization, is an act of immediate Knowledge-Awareness because Pure Being can not be reached by steps or by means of supports, nor can Pure Being be attained in actuation-process."

Raphael

CONTENTS

PREFACE

The most difficult problem discussed by philosophers down through the ages is that of Being and non-being, of One and many and, as a consequence, the question of generation.

Is the Absolute Being Unity, Duality or Non-duality?

Is the world of names and forms created *ex-nihilo*, is it manifested or emanated? And again is it real or unreal or, paradoxically, both the one and the other? From Thales to Pythagoras, from Plato to Plotinus and down to recent philosophers these problems have received answers, at times acceptable, sometimes incomprehensible and other times unacceptable.

What has the *Advaita* Philosophy, presented by Gauḍapāda and Śaṃkarācārya and re-proposed here by Raphael, got to say with regard to these matters?

We may say that this doctrine, which is of a deeply philosophical and metaphysical nature, not only gives an answer that is new to the West but it also points out the pathway (*Asparśa-vāda*) by which to achieve the Identity of the being with Being.

Raphael, using a conceptual methodology in keeping with the characteristics of the Western mind, helps us to understand the 'vision' of Gauḍapāda and Śaṃkarācārya who, solidly established in metaphysics, show how the Supreme Being is pure actuation which excludes not only multiplicity, duality and ontological unity, but also all passages from potentiality to act. To speak of the ever-present and infinite Being in terms of even theoretical phases is impossible. The Ever-Present has no history, no actuation, no motion because It has no generation (*ajāti*).

Pure Being is what It is, It is not what was nor what will be. And if at times one speaks of 'three levels' of Being this is done only to help the minds of men—which are made up of *aporias* and *abaliety*—and only with a view to free them from the illusion of 'two' and 'one'. 'Multiplicity', 'two' and 'one', that is, pluralism, dualism and the mathematical one, exasperate and disappoint us because unconsciously we tend towards the Non-duality (Pure Being) or the Absolute which is ever present and makes thought and phenomenal appearance possible.

If the Absolute is 'that which is free from relations, that is, exists and is what It is, without any need to be in relationship with anything else, or what is fully sufficient, self-sufficient independently of any other thing or reality', then Gauḍapāda, Śaṃkarācārya and Raphael indicate the true metaphysical pathway leading to the realization of the unqualified Absolute Being. *Asparśa* means, in fact, 'free from relations', from connections with other things; it means self-sufficiency, that is, non-generation (*a-jāti*).

This book, which we present above all to those who are 'lovers of knowledge' (Philosophers), is composed of a series of questions and answers regarding some aspects of Non-duality (*Advaita*) discussed by Raphael, a Researcher-Philosopher who has achieved *Asparśavāda* (i.e. the pathway of no support) and is keeping alive *Advaita* Tradition which has had in Gauḍapāda and Śaṃkarācārya its most representative 'revivers' both from the point of view of Realization and Doctrine; in fact they codified in their writings the fundamental principles of *Asparśavāda* and *Advaita Vedānta.*[1]

Gauḍapāda's *Asparśavāda* and Śaṃkarācārya's *Advaita Vedānta* represent the crowning of Raphael's research. In them he found the statements of his metaphysical conclusions, confirmed later on also by *Orphism, Platonism, Neo-platonism, Qabbālāh* and *Hermetism.* After years of patient research, reflection, meditation and investigation Raphael achieved a cognitive-consciential synthesis of the various branches of tradition, expressions of that *Philosophia perennis* which contains universal truths no people or age may claim as its own.

---

1. Cp. the *Māṇḍūkya Upaniṣad* with the *Kārikās* by Gauḍapāda, Śaṃkara's commentary and notes by Raphael, Edizioni Āśram Vidyā, Roma.

For Raphael, philosophy means total knowledge-realization, identity with the cognitive aspect: knowledge, knower and known must coincide perfectly. The true philosopher or Lover of *Sophia*-Knowledge is he who shows a coherence between thought and being so as to become a 'life style'. Thus, he who 'knows' is a Teacher not only of thought but also of life. This has brought Raphael close to the conception of the Greek and Eastern philosophers whose philosophy is above all self-revelation or an unveiling of the knowledge sought and not the satisfaction of the childish desire of a capricious mind seeking gratification in questioning.

Measuring oneself with the Absolute, with the Whole (as Plato says), with Being rather than becoming, implies a precise subsequent change of all the usual points of view, of the meaning of life itself and a new hierarchy of values.

The knowledge of the Whole, according to Plato, requires 'breaking chains', requires 'ascesis', demands 'dedicating one's whole self', a change of life and, as Raphael says, 'a transformation of consciousness'.

It is important to underline two points in order to understand the true meaning of what is written in this book:

— in these 'dialogues' Raphael discusses and offers a solution to a series of themes that go beyond geographical and ideological bounds thus becoming the heritage of the whole humanity.

— Raphael's answers are given in the light of *Advaitavāda* using conceptual terms in keeping with the Western mind and its particular modes of philosophical reception.

1

NON-DUALISM, DUALISM AND MONISM

Q.[1] What do the following terms, often used by the *Vedānta:* dualism, monism, monotheism and non-dualism, mean?

A. Every philosophical or cosmological vision which affirms two opposing and *irreducible* principles to explain Reality is a dualistic vision.

Philosophical dualism is an answer to the problem of Being, which is considered double, being made of matter and spirit, of ego and non-ego, eternally in opposition and independent of one another.

Religious dualism, on the other hand, opposes two principles in eternal conflict and *antinomia.* It explains the presence of evil in the world and existence of the world itself as the outcome of the constant struggle between two eternal principles, the one called Good, the other Evil. These two opposing principles are often personified as God and Satan: the former the expression of Good, the latter of Evil.

Every dualistic concept—whether philosophical or religious—recognizes, in other words, two distinct causes, or two independent *substances,* to use the words of Aristotle, which due to their very nature can never meet, never relate or resolve themselves. This implies that—at the manifest level—all contradictions, all antinomies, which arise and exist, can never be resolved. Two parallel lines, however much they be drawn out, can never meet.

Evil, being an absolute Reality, just like Good, can never be overcome by Good, and vice-versa.

Dualism presents from the onset contradictions that cannot be solved or supported.

Philosophical, religious or cosmological monism conceives

1. Q. = Question, A. = Answer.

the multiplicity of manifestations as the effect of a sole *substance.* It is obviously opposed to both dualism and pluralism. For pluralism Reality is made not of two but of several *substances.*

Monism can be compared to the mathematical one from which all numbers derive. The multiplicity of numbers is simply the multiplication of the one.

There is the materialistic monism for which only one *substance* exists; matter, and all other categories, including spirit and even the consciousness, are the epiphenomena of the one material *substance.* And there is—in total opposition to the former theory—spiritualistic monism, for which all can be traced back to a single *substance* which is the Spirit.

For monism every existing element—of any type and at any level whatsoever—is real, because it represents the emanation from or multiplication of the one sole Reality. From this standpoint we might say that monism is pantheistic. Thus, within the field of monism we have to include Spinoza's pantheism which states the oneness of *substance* and the identity of God and nature.

In realistic pantheism all antinomies, like good and evil for example, although they go back to original unity, must be considered real and therefore they cannot—on the plane of manifestation—dissolve or transcend. Evil, ignorance, unhappiness, limit, etc., are universal realities about which nothing can be done by man, because they are consubstantial with the One. We can say that the One contains within Itself the dialectics of opposites. All manifested effects, polar or dual as they may be, are contained in the First Cause. This means, naturally, attributing the good-evil principle itself to the One-Principle.

Q. What is monotheism?

A. Monotheism—typical of religion—affirms the existence of a sole Divinity. It is the opposite of polytheism and fetichism.

Some religions admit of a number of gods to control the laws of the universe as second principles. However, as they are made to derive from a sole supreme God who includes them all, these religions may be considered as being fundamentally monotheistic.

Here too emerges the impossibility of overcoming consciential, psychological and formal dualism because this is emanated, or created, by the One God.

If the world *is* Real, then it is not possible to change, transform or redeem it. It will never be possible to rectify or redeem what really is.

Q. What is Non-dualism then?

A. Non-dualism is neither monism nor monotheism and, of course, it is not dualism.

Since monism might be compared to the mathematical one and the latter to multiplicity, in order to avoid misunderstandings the term "non-dual" is used. In other words, the unity that is not multipliable, which does not generate or is not mathematical is called non-dual. This non-dual unity may be considered as belonging to the metaphysical order.

From the mathematical one, which is the generating principle of the total series of numbers, we arrive at the metaphysical One which is beyond all possible numerical nomenclature.

If for monism and dualism the universe-object is created by or emanates from the First Cause, for non-dualism the universe-object is neither creation nor emanation, but a simple *māyā-phenomenon* shown upon the screen of the universe or of the individual by the projecting power of what we call 'mind'. Thus, for example, our dreams or imagination—whether sleeping or waking—are simply *māyika projections* that have no absolute reality and therefore may dissolve at any moment. The universe is a *continuum-discontinuum* that can be resolved and transcended. It is not, therefore, a creation—in the sense generally given to this term—because the Supreme Reality, being complete in itself, does not *need* to create. Nor is it an emanation because the Supreme Reality does not exhaust itself in the manifest, nor does it transform itself to become other than what it is.

An individual, planetary or cosmic body-form is the effect of a movement which, were it to cease, would cause the form to disappear.

The universe is a 'dream' (but this term must not be taken literally). We have a body and we are moving, because we are dreaming. If we wish to emerge from all apparent consciential, psychological and formal dualism, we must wake up and stop the movement. It is not Reality in itself that causes dualism, but it is the 'movement' of the *jīva* (the living soul) which in turn is a *projection* of the Absolute Self. Likewise, when we are in a train it is not the landscape outside that moves but the train and we, and because of *māyā* we attribute the movement to the trees and the fields. From this point of view, the mathematical one and dualism are not absolute realities for non-dualism. They are not *substances* but *appearances* and as such they can be transcended and solved. 'Evil', but also 'good', is not a reality in itself, it is not *substance* but *appearance*, a particular *movement*, but it can be solved and transcended. The universe of names and forms is not something in itself, it is not a reality that lives by its own life, it is not Being, it is simply movement (apparent if seen from the point of view of the Absolute Reality) which causes non-substantial event-things. Our nightly dreams are not absolute realities, are not eternal, are not *substantial*, have no origin and nowhere to go. They are only phenomena projected by the mind upon the immobile screen of our being. To say that a dream *is* the individual himself or that the individual *exhausts* himself in the dream, or again, that the dream is eternal and immortal means pushing things too far. What causes this vital 'appearance', these worlds—apparently solid and immortal—is *māyā*.

Between the Real and the non-real (which appears real) stands *māyā*. It is sufficient to eliminate *māyā* to discover a sole *substance*, that is, the Supreme Reality always identical to Itself.

Q. But can *māyā* be studied empirically and consciously?

A. When we want to study our dreams consciously an unexpected event occurs: we awaken and wakefulness dispels our dream as if by magic. The ego and the non-ego of the dream (duality) disappear.

When we wish to examine empirically the snake we have seen instead of a rope, the snake disappears and we are left with the rope.

When we try to examine *māyā* consciously, this disappears

taking with it all dualism and *antinomia*, and in its place we find Being, Reality and the Absolute Constant.

Māyā cannot be observed or analyzed empirically because it is not reality.

Wanting to 'see' or 'trace' *māyā* is like looking in the air for the trace left by a passing bird, says Śaṃkara. Though not seen, it can be resolved and transcended by means of *vidyā*, metaphysical knowledge.

We ascribe reality and truth to things - objects because we believe them to be real and true, capable of granting satisfaction and fulfilment. In doing so we become alienated as our completeness and happiness are dependent on something other than ourselves. But the 'other' is a mere fancy, a non-substance unable, for its particular nature, to grant *pax profunda*. For Non-duality the basic error is believing in things that, all considered, are not. In order to eliminate this error, due to *avidyā* or invalid knowledge (opinion-*doxa*), we need *vidyā* or noetic knowledge.

Q. We might say that the world of names and forms can be transcended and solved by the power of Knowledge (*vidyā*), might we not?

A. As long as the 'snake' is seen and perpetuated by the projective power of the mind, it is considered as existing, real and substantial. Only when we awaken and recognize the true 'rope-being', the 'snake' disappears without leaving a trace. Thus, for Non-dualism the world of names and forms is real and non-real, depending upon the point of view from which it is observed and considered.

Q. Has the metaphysical One been seen and pointed out only by the *Vedic* Tradition?

A. The *Vedic* Tradition is only a branch of the One Tradition. The Tradition of the *Sacred Mysteries* of ancient Greece—above all the Orphic Tradition—recognized the metaphysical One, even though this truth was revealed only at the very last levels of the Great Mysteries.

It is sufficient to go back to Plotinus, who took up and gave new life to the ancient Mysteric Tradition. He says:

".... the One must be without form. But if it is without form it is not a substance, for a substance must be something particular, something, that is, defined and limited; but it is impossible to apprehend the One as a particular thing, for then it would not be a principle, but only that particular thing which you said it was. But if all things are in that which is generated [from the One], which of the things in it are you going to say that the One is? Since it is none of them, it can only be said to be beyond them. But these things are beings, and being: so it is 'beyond being'. This phrase 'beyond being' does not mean that it is a particular thing—for it makes no positive statement about it—and it does not say its name, but all it implies is that it is 'not this'. But if this is what the phrase does, it in no way comprehends the One. It would be absurd to seek to comprehend that boundless nature, for anyone who wants to do this has put himself out of the way of following at all, even the least distance, in its traces; but just as he who wishes to see the intelligible nature will contemplate what is beyond the perceptible if he has no mental image of the perceptible, so he who wishes to contemplate what is beyond the intelligible will contemplate it when he has let all the intelligible go. He will learn that it is by means of the intelligible, but what it is like by letting the intelligible go. But this 'what it is like' must indicate that it is 'not like', for there is no 'being like' in what is not a 'something'. But we in our travail do not know what we ought to say, and are speaking of what cannot be spoken, and give it a name because we want to indicate it to ourselves as best we can."

".... but that has no shape, not even intelligible shape.... It is not therefore something or qualified or quantitative or intellect or soul; it is not in movement or at rest, not in place, not in time, but 'itself by itself of single form', or rather formless, being before all form, before movement and before rest, for these pertain to being and are what make it many. .... 'One' must be understood in a larger sense than that in which a unity and a point are unified.... And it must be understood as infinite not because its size and number cannot be measured or counted but because its power cannot be comprehended. For when you think of it as Intellect or God, it is more."[1]

(*Enneads*: V, 5, vi; VI, 9, iii-vi)

1. All passages from the *Enneads* quoted in this book are taken from *Plotinus*, The Joeb Classical Library, Harvard University Press, Cambridge, Mass.

2

REAL AND NON-REAL

Q. What is meant by real and non-real in Śaṃkara's *Advaita* and Gauḍapāda's *Asparśavāda*?

A. The problem of real and non-real, of Being and non-being is very complex, therefore one gets different answers depending upon the point of view from which one looks at the question. We are obliged, therefore, to give an example.

Let us take a body-form, a cloud in the sky, for example. Is it real or non-real? Is a dream real or non-real? Some hold that it is real, others that it is not, and others still that it is both real and non-real (*sat-asat*). It all depends upon one's point of view, on one's own position of consciousness or the particular system of co-ordinates which one is using to analyse things.

Those who hold that a cloud in the sky—by way of example—is real, trust in a knowledge of an empirical, perceptive-sensory kind, in knowledge by means of the five senses. If an object can be seen, touched, tasted they say then it cannot be held to be unreal or an illusion. What can be touched and seen *is there*, it occupies a place, it lasts in time and can be observed and experienced by all.

Those who hold that things do not exist conceive reality as non-sensory, non-material and non-substantial. For them—see pure idealism and acosmism—ontological reality is exclusively ideal. Things enjoy no reality of their own and the Spirit-Being cannot be the object of sensorial knowledge, because it is beyond the senses. Therefore pure Being exists while all that is not Being is unreality.

Those who maintain that things are real and unreal (*sat-asat*)—synthesizing the other two points of view—have a particular conception of reality which must be examined because it is not as superficial and reductive as the first two concepts.

Let us see what kind of reasoning lies behind this third point of view. If our senses see, touch and perceive we cannot obviously say that they touch and see 'nothing'. Nothing—like the horns of a hare or a barren woman's child—cannot be perceived, touched or seen by any of the senses, however perfect they may be. Therefore we cannot support the theory of those who hold that the senses perceive 'nothing' or that things do not exist. However, at this stage we must get into the matter more and make a number of points.

To think that nothing exists beyond objectivity because the senses or figurative thinking cannot perceive it means either being absolutist or onesided or else it means refusing to investigate and find a solution to the problem. Things—a cloud in the sky—*appear* and *disappear*, they are and they are not, they come and go, they are born and they die. In other words, they change continually. The senses themselves that touch and see soon cease to touch and see because the objects disappear.

On the other hand, it is legitimate to ask: what do our eyes really see? What our retina perceives as an image is a series of luminous vibrations which come from things outside of us. When our senses see or touch things, they are not seeing-touching the things *in themselves* but rather their images given to the retina or to the tactile organs by their vibrations. The mind—as the sixth sense—translates and interprets the images obtained by the retina but not the thing *in itself*. Our truth springs from the interpretation or translation of a 'sensorial image'.

Besides—as we have already mentioned—the vibrations caused by things are not constant, are not absolute, because they are subject to endless vibratory modifications and the image we perceive, as a result, is altered too. Matter undergoes continuous change, it is a force-field and therefore it is impossible to grasp the thing in itself.

From this point of view then, a cloud in the sky is certainly perceived, but a moment later one must admit that it is no longer perceived. This is a matter of fact, this is evident. It is an empirical fact of experience. Therefore, how can we say that things are real and absolute? A true and genuine reality must always be seen, perceived and found, within and outside of time, and in every place. If the said reality appears to our senses and then disappears like a flash or a mirage, to what extent can we say that it is real?

To consider absolute-real what appears and disappears inevitably means wanting to force matters. On the other hand, the empiricists do not accept dreams as real, and yet dreams are perceived by the senses just like any other thing.

We err when we say we know things because—as we have said above—we only know the image we have of things. And we even know that this image is subject to alteration and change in time and space.

Reality, fragmented into indefinable and fleeting phenomena, does not guarantee the stability and certainty of knowledge, but leaves it a prey to gnawing relativism, incapable of determination. Thought dies in anguish, losing itself in frustrating *aporias* and contradictions.

We must also say that the empiricists recognize all this, but as they do not wish to arrive at the point reached by the pure idealists, and as they are attached to their own point of view, they are obliged to make the following paradoxical statement: Reality is appearance, relativity and change. But this statement does not seem to be reasonable for the simple reason that if everything is relative and changing then even the statement 'all is relative' is relative.

If an entity is relative and not constant, how can it state an absolute reality or a reality of any other order and dimension? In other words, a relative entity can only state relative truths. Thus, what the empiricist sees and touches sensorially is not Reality with a capital R, but a simple phenomenon that appears and disappears. However, a phenomenon is not pure nothing, it is the effect of a particular movement which determines the apparition of a body-form, of an event that is not 'substance'. This movement, in turn, is an effect because its existence is the outcome of relation.

If the empiricist is obliged to consider all as relative and non-permanent, then his idea coincides, in part, with the *Advaita* point of view, that is, with a point of view which is apparently the very opposite of his own. Opposites meet, when one tries to really understand them.

At this point, let us examine the point of view mentioned before which states that only Being exists and not becoming.

When examining the empiricists' view, we stated that it is impossible to reject things altogether. However, we concluded that what we know is not reality but phenomenon-becoming or the mental and individual *interpretation* of the said phenomenon. And if all we see and touch is phenomenon-movement, there must be a factor upon which such phenomenon-movement depends. It is not possible to see phenomenon-effects that do not depend upon causes-principles. Becoming, being *abaliety*, cannot depend upon that very same becoming.

How can we know the Being that lies behind the phenomenon and behind mental-sensory interpretation? That Being which the empiricists would like to touch and see as if it were a phenomenon-object?

If a phenomenal *object* can be seen and touched with equally relative, phenomenal and objectual tools, Being as pure *Subject* can only be known through Being, through consciousness of self as Subject-Being, in so far as Being is not an 'object'.

When we eliminate or transcend phenomenon-becoming, Being reveals Itself in Its absolute reality and *aseity*.

If one can know the relative by putting oneself upon the plane of relativity and upon that of simple interpretation, then one also can know the Being by putting oneself upon the plane of *identity*. Western philosophy, in general, has not solved the problem of the knowledge of Being, because it has always put itself upon a dual plane, even when believing to state the Oneness of reality.

Q. Can Being be experienced?

A. Being can be experienced only upon a plane of identity. Thus traditional or realizative Philosophy proposes the knowledge of Being through the *realization* of Being.

Q. So, *Advaita* has something in common with both the Philosophy of Being and that of becoming?

A. Yes, because it includes three levels or stages of Reality (*satya*) in its vision:

-*pāramārthika*	=	pure or absolute reality
-*vyāvahārika*	=	empirical or phenomenal reality
-*prātibhāsika*	=	illusory existence.

Pāramārthika is that Reality which cannot be contradicted by any other reality or existential experience, because there is no 'second' to which it can relate.

Vyāvahārika is the empirical reality of the five senses. This is the phenomenal reality which is perceived in the world of names and forms and which can be contradicted by other realities and experiences.

Prātibhāsika is illusion, like the illusion we have when we see a mirage or two moons instead of one.

Asat, non-being in the strictest sense, is the non-existent, the non-real, like the hare's horns and the barren woman's child. But compared with *pāramārthika* Reality, one may say that even *vyāvahārika* truth, the empirical truth, is illusory because it is non-permanent, non-constant.

Thus the ultimate conclusion of *Advaita* is that Being and becoming are both dialectical 'moments' of the Absolute or non-qualified supreme Reality (*nirguṇa*).

3

AJĀTIVĀDA AND ASPARŚAVĀDA

Q. In the *Māṇḍūkyakārikā* by Gauḍapāda *Ajātivāda* and *Asparśavāda* are spoken of. But what are *Ajātivāda* and *Asparśavāda*?

A. In order to understand this metaphysical vision it is necessary first of all to comprehend the philosophical attitude of the *Vedānta* in general.

In the Hindu Tradition, connected to the *Vedas*, there are six *darśanas* which, rather than Western kind of philosophical systems—that are the result of mere individual speculations of single philosophers using the *manas*-mind—represent 'points of view', 'visions' or 'perspectives' regarding *Vedic* teaching. It must also be kept in mind that in the East philosophy and religion—in the purest sense—are united; philosophy is a 'way of being', it is a consciential and not a simple mental attitude. In other words, philosophy implies realization: *to know is to be*. Therefore when we speak of philosophy and metaphysics we intend them in their purest traditional sense. We could also speak of realizative philosophy and metaphysics; those of Pythagoras, Plato, Plotinus, for example, are realizative philosophies because they involve the *very consciousness* of the being, not merely its mind as a simple discoursive factor.

The *darśanas*, being points of view, to grasp the Real start from certain *perspectives* that may be more or less complete, inclusive and universal. Thus, for example, the *Sāṃkhya-darśana* (*sāṃkhya* means 'numeration') starts from the empirical outlook rather than from the metaphysical one; it counts all the 'modifications' that substance undergoes from the primordial matter (*prakṛti*)—under the impulse of *puruṣa*—to gross physical matter. Without any doubt, this is a valid point of view which considers becoming rather than Being. But, we must point out, it is not a materialistic *darśana*, because the aim of the *Sāṃkhya* is to free *puruṣa* from the modifications of *prakṛti. Puruṣa* and *prakṛti* correspond in an approximate manner to essence and substance, or to spirit and matter, in the Western sense. We may say, however, that it is a dualistic point of view in that it presents the two poles, *puruṣa* and *prakṛti*, as co-eternal. This does not mean that it opposes monism; only that Kapila, codifier of the *Sāṃkhya*, begins his treatise on the One when it is already differentiated or polarized. For example, we can study dense-physical matter from the molecular, atomic or sub-atomic point of view. It is obvious that, according to the branch of studies, the point of view changes, although there is no contradiction between one field and the others.

If, therefore, we grasp the fact that the *darśanas* are 'points of view', we realize that the various authors, codifiers of the *darśanas*, 'saw' Reality from different consciential viewpoints which are the states of consciousness reached by them, the positions realized by them. Gauḍapāda—to use the analogy mentioned before—goes beyond the substantial texture, beyond the molecular condition, beyond the atomic state, to touch the state of elementary essence, beyond all manifested factors. It is obvious, therefore, that Gauḍapāda (codifier of *Ajātivāda*) and Kapila (codifier of the *Sāṃkhyavāda*), starting from different standpoints, arrive at different conclusions which are not opposed or excluding each other. We should underline, however, that the molecular point of view, compared with the elementary one, is characterized by its relativity and non-absoluteness. The molecules are *born*, they *develop* and *disappear*, while the elementary state subsists. And indeed, the molecules dissolve into the elementary state because they are non-absolute, non-constant. The mass (body-compound) dissolves into energy. In this perspective, and transposing the whole on to a metaphysical level, *Ajātivāda* presents the characteristic of absoluteness and universality as compared with *Sāṃkhyavāda* which, however valid, is nonetheless reductive.

Q. Did Gauḍapāda 'see' Reality in its ultimate non-determination?

A. Yes. Gauḍapāda, by adopting the perspective of the Absolute as such, or of the pure Being (*Advaita*) was able to say, rightly, that in It there is no birth or generation or modification. Pure Being was never born, therefore it cannot die or cease to be. And if it was not born there can be no *real* manifestation. If the Absolute Being cannot *transform Itself* or become multiple then, Gauḍapāda asks, what is that we see? This is the admirable metaphysical or *Advaita* perspective of Gauḍapāda's *Ajātivāda*.

The atom on the gross-physical level is the first determination from which the various physical compounds arise, but beyond the atom there is no body-form, there is only 'formless' energy; in other words, there is no manifestation as we know it. Gauḍapāda, by going on to the metaphysical level, went beyond the first Determination-Being from which the formal universes arise, but beyond the first Determination there is no universe, no form, no compound, either atomic or molecular. We can say that beyond the first Determination there is the non-qualified (*nirguṇa*), non-caused state.

The *Ajātivāda*, seen within the perspective of the manifest—and the manifest includes the gross-physical, the subtle and the causal-germinal states—, might seem a logical absurdity and a pragmatic impossibility, but this is understandable. The identification and assimilation with one consciential state excludes the comprehension of another state. If the individual, for example, identifies with the formal becoming (dualism in general), he will never be able to understand a point of view that goes beyond duality. If the individual identifies with his physical body (substance), he will never be able to understand himself in terms of pure Being that is never born, never grows and is never caused. A metaphysical 'Vision' implies going beyond the space-time-cause perspective; space, time and cause are *determinations* inherent in form, in compounds, in phenomena. The more the consciousness identifies with the formal aspect, the greater will be the difficulty of going beyond this perspective.

Q. Gauḍapāda also spoke of *Asparśavāda*. What is this?

A. All told, *Ajātivāda* and *Asparśavāda* are one and the same thing. *A-jāti* means non-generation or non-birth and *jāti* means birth, generation—taken to mean the passage from Non-being to Being. *Asparśa* is the *yoga* or the *path* that leads to the non-generated state of pure Being. Besides, *sparśa* means contact, relation and *a-sparśa* means non-contact, non-relation. Now the Absolute Being is often considered as without relation, without contact with anything because, being one without a second (*Advaita*), It could establish a relation or have a contact with nothing.

Q. *Asparśavāda* is also called the path without supports, why?

A. The support of the 'ego', which is relativity, is based on the form-manifestation aspect and on the qualities (*guṇas*) which the substance expresses. *Asparśa*, being a *vāda* of a metaphysical nature, tends to remove all *supports* inherent in being. By eliminating all formal supports the 'reflection or ray of consciousness' falls into *That* which is pure Being without supports, without relations or duality. From a philosophical point of view we could say that *Asparśavāda* tends to eliminate the time-space-cause support which is the qualification of the phenomenon, but not of the noumenon.

Q. Is that why this path appears difficult?

A. Yes, because it is a realizative metaphysics that tends to solve all the determinations of Being. The 'ego', in that it is a manifested *object*, fears its *annihilation* because it cannot imagine itself without form, without time or determination. On the other hand this is right: the molecular 'ego' could never conceive itself as an atomic self because this belongs to another dimension.

Gauḍapāda in chapter III, *kārikā* 39, says[1] :

> "This *yoga* called *asparśa* is very difficult for many *yogins* to understand because they, feeling fear where there is none, are afraid of it."

And Śaṃkara explaining this *kārikā* declares that this metaphysical *yoga* is hard to be attained by *yogins* lacking in true knowledge. "The *yogins*" says Śaṃkara "are afraid (of this *yoga*) while they should not be. The non-discriminating fear,

1. Cp. *Māṇḍūkyakārikā*, Edizioni Āśram Vidyā, 1981.

while practising this *yoga*, the extinction of their individuality, although (*asparśa*) is beyond all fear."

And again, in *kārikā* 2, chapter IV, it is stated:

> "I bow to this *yoga*—taught by the Scriptures—well known as *asparśa*, free from relations, beneficial, generator of beatitude for all beings and free from oppositions and contradictions. . . ."

Why free from contradictions? Because a contradiction or an opposition can be had only on the plane of duality. An empirical experience can be contradicted by another empirical experience. For example, the experience of waking by dreaming, that of dreaming by waking, and both are contradicted by deep dreamless sleep. But in *Turīya* (the metaphysical state of pure Being) there can be no contradiction, because in it the experiencer and the experienced, or subject and object, do not exist.

Q. Thus from the point of view of the Absolute nothing is born?

A. From the point of view of the Absolute there can be no birth or death, transformation or modification. From the point of view of the sun the earthly dawn and sunset are not absolute realities, and indeed they do not exist at all. There is no movement in the sun that can cause dawn and sunset (duality). There is no movement in pure Being that can cause birth and death.

Q. By what means did Gauḍapāda arrive at this truth?

A. By means of Knowledge, intuitive discernment and naturally by relying upon the authority of the *Śruti*.

Q. But what kind of Knowledge?

A. The *Vedānta*, and therefore Gauḍapāda, proposes various kinds of Knowledge: a strictly illusory one, an empirical mediated one given by the *manas* (projective mind) which knows only the object-form, and the immediate kind or 'Knowledge of identity'. In other words, one must distinguish between what is simple sensorial opinion and what is true and authentic Knowledge-Science which reveals Reality, Truth as it is.

Q. In synthesis, therefore, what are the postulates upon which the Vision of the *Ajātivāda* rests?

A. There is an unchanging, eternal, ever-present and actual Reality without generation and extinction, devoid of cause-effect and of space-time, having no contradiction, One without a second. As Reality is constant and perfect unity, all that is differentiation, multiplicity, fleetingness and change cannot be Ultimate and Supreme Reality but only *appearance*, representation which may seem to be real if observed from the point of view of opinion. The snake we see in place of the rope may be real as long as we believe it to be so, but at the touch of Superior Knowledge the snake proves to be a simple superimposition veiling the true identity of the rope.

The world of names and forms is nothing but mere appearance, phenomenon which appears and disappears; it is a *continuum-discontinuum* which may be interrupted at any given moment when, that is, the Supreme Knowledge of Identity (*Parā Vidyā*) becomes evident within ourselves. On the other hand, becoming offers a knowledge which *is not*, an unstable, uncertain knowledge, in other words, a non-knowledge. According to Gauḍapāda all pairs of opposites, not being absolute, dissolve into the One-without-a-Second.

4

PARMENIDES AND HIS VISION

Q. Which Western Vision can we consider nearest to Gauḍapāda's *Ajātivāda*?

A. That of Parmenides. For him too the teaching is based upon the above mentioned postulates. For the Eleatic there is only one Way (*hodós*) which solves the existential enigma, a way which 'lies far away from the path beaten by men', a pathway which leads to that *doorway* which transcends Day and Night (duality), and reveals the a-spatial Reality, a way which is '... devoid of temporal end'. Parmenides' Way is also the one which Yājñavalkya describes in the *Bṛhadāraṇyaka Upaniṣad* (IV, iv, 8):

> "A narrow way laid down in ancient times, leading to me, by me it was discovered. By it the strong, knowers of *Brahman*, freed from this one ascend to the high celestial world."

Parmenides' is undoubtedly an initiatory pathway and the most modern and attentive exegesis seems to be orientated towards this conclusion.

Jaeger too agrees with this thesis when he writes: "Before this super-human prelude (speaking of Parmenides' proem) nobody can believe that the philosopher wished to place himself in the limelight. The vision of this mysterious event in the kingdom of light is an authentic religious experience: the experience of human eyes which turn towards the hidden truth, so that the whole life is transfigured." But this kind of religiousness "must be sought in the religiousness of the Initiations and of the Mysteries. Parmenides was able to grasp this because in Southern Italy, in his day, these ideas were widespread."

For the Eleatic there exists, therefore, a sole Way and a sole Reality: Being in that It *is*. It is unity, actuality, permanency, not subject either to birth or death, one and indivisible. Only that Being which *is and does not become*, which is complete, ever present, identical to Itself is necessarily a Reality which fills everything.

> "Being ungenerated, it is also imperishable, entire, sole, still and endless. It never was nor will be because it is now whole, one, continuous. In fact, what origin can you wish to seek for It? How and where could It have been born? Of non-being I shall not allow you to speak or think. In fact, what is not cannot be uttered or thought of. And even so, what need could have urged It, which rises from nothing, to be born, before or after? Therefore it is necessary for It to be either wholly or not at all. And never shall the force of true conviction allow that anything different from It be born of Being."

It can only be known through the mediation of that noetic (immediate understanding and, according to Stefanini's exegesis, 'contemplative ecstasy') and epistemological knowledge that reveals only the supreme intelligible. Knowledge is that "...upon which Persuasion walks, and Persuasion is the follower of truth".

For Parmenides too the world of names and forms (the empirical world) is simple *appearance*, and is presented (as in Gauḍapāda) as a dialectical moment and not as absolute necessity.

> "Therefore they will all be just *names*, which mortals have established, convinced that they are true: birth and death, being and non-being, change of place and mutation of brilliant colour."

Becoming, contingent and change seem, from a false standpoint, to be and exist.

> "But from this way [of opinion, which believes that things that are not are] of research remove your thought.... This cosmic order, *apparent* as it is, I shall reveal to you in detail, so that no opinion of any mortal may overcome you."

Aristotle in his *De Coel* (1298 b. 14) states:

> "Some of them [he is speaking of Parmenides and Melissos] denied the existence of generation and corruption altogether, saying in fact that nothing among the entities is either generated or dies, but it only seems so to us."

The intellect that does not base itself upon Pure Being, unable to offer true Reality, projects and represents only names, simple words which the 'doxophile' men—to say it with Plato—take for absolute, supreme Truth. In this sense the following passage from Plato is emblematic:

> "And would it not perhaps be an adequate defence if we were to reply that he who truly loves knowledge should naturally tend towards Being, and refusing to be satisfied by the multiplicity of the single objects—*they are nothing but content of opinion*—walk straight ahead without losing courage or betraying his love before having grasped the nature of each thing in itself with that part of his Soul whose activity is indeed to grasp the essence of things—It having the same nature—, and with this part of his Soul approaching and uniting himself with Being in Itself, generating understanding and truth, succeed in knowing in actuality, live a true life, feed upon true nourishment, and thus finish to suffer, but not before, the pangs of childbirth?"
>
> (*Republic:* 490 b)

We should furthermore point out that Parmenides—notwithstanding the different opinion of a number of exegetics—does not entirely negate the world of *doxa* (the empirical world), he simply sets it in its proper place as 'appearance', as phenomenon, because it is resolved and transcended by the superior and supreme certainty of Being. The fact that the Goddess explains to Parmenides the structure and the workings of the world-*doxa* means that this must have a 'degree' of recognition, because there can be no talk of nothing, of things that do not exist, of the barren woman's child or the hare's horns, to use Gauḍapāda's and Śaṃkara's expressions.

"However, you will also learn how appearance must be judged by he who in all directions investigates everything."

On the other hand, Parmenides himself says that of non-being as such there is nothing to be said:

"... in fact one can neither utter nor think of what is not."

The Eleatic contests only those who take the relative for the Absolute, becoming for Being, opinion (*doxa*) for truth (*alétheia*); and again, he is opposed to those who place Being and becoming upon the same plane.

Being is the metaphysical basis of the 'world of names' or of becoming and this finds its justifications in that, not being able to justify itself. This is how Aristotle puts it:

"Now, if nothing existed beyond the single things, the intelligible would not exist, therefore all would be sensorially perceivable and as a result there would be no science, unless one wishes to state that sensation be science. Besides, there would be nothing eternal or immobile; but if nothing eternal existed, becoming itself would be impossible."

(*Metaphysics*: B, 4, 999 b)

Thus the world of *doxa* is appearance, similar to a dream when compared with the supreme Reality of Being which is its very basis.

"Men", writes H. Schwabl (*Sein und Doxa bei Parmenides—Being and Doxa in Parmenides*) "err only when they retain the *apparent* to be eternal and they consider it as Being ... they are instead right with *doxa* when they acknowledge its fleeting and conditioned value...."

All pairs of opposites, such as Light and Dark, for Schwabl "may be unified in the superior unity of Being" (*Ibid.*).

The things we see with our sensory eyes are all 'names' which appear and disappear, and are annulled before the fullness and majesty of that Being which *is and does not become.*

We can say that this vision is in line with that of Gauḍapāda and therefore with that of the *Upaniṣads.*

Q. It seems, however, that Parmenides depicts Being as a sphere, while Gauḍapāda speaks of *Brahman* as infinite, bodyless and beyond categories that belong to manifestation.

A. This is right as far as Gauḍapāda is concerned, but to understand Parmenides it is necessary to get into the spirit of his vision rather than dwell upon the face value of his words.

In ancient Greece the figure of the sphere was considered the symbol of perfection, of completeness, of unity, etc.; whereas all that was indefinite, formless, vague, nebulous, etc. was considered to be lacking in perfection and devoid of unity. Roundness gives us the impression of 'fullness', of self-sufficiency, of completeness as well as harmony and beauty, and as completeness it transcends all categories and all temporal and spatial empirical determinations. It stands for the pure metaphysical quality of the self-shining Being and its ideal circularness can 'extend itself' as far as the infinite because it represents the emanation of the Pole-point or of the centre, always identical to itself.

Thus, when one wished, for example, to speak of things in terms of perfection, unity, fullness, stability, etc., one referred to that 'yardstick of measurement' represented by the sphere. Plato too—like the *Upaniṣads*—speaks of Being as a shining Sun. These are empirical or analogical images the true value of which must be sought in the metaphysical dimension.

Parmenides speaks also of 'round truth':

> "You must learn to know all things, both the immovable spirit of the well-rounded truth, and the opinions of mortals wherein there dwells no legitimate credibility."

Now, were we to interpret literally the expression 'well-rounded truth' we would come up against a logical absurdity. But, if we enter into the spirit of Parmenides' thinking, of his day and of Tradition, then all will appear to be clear to us. 'Spherical truth' gives us the idea of perfect truth, of perfect knowledge, of an indubitable truth of such stability that nobody may shake or destroy, as against the truth of men which is instead simple opinion and therefore nebulous, vague, non-definite truth and unstable knowledge.[1]

Here are a number of *kārikās* by Gauḍapāda[2] which require no explanation:

> "Now I shall speak of That which has no limit, never born and which is in constant equilibrium, and hear how it is impossible for anything to be born, though it may seem to have been born."
>
> "The creation which—with the aid of the examples of earth, gold, sparks, etc.—, has been explained in various ways, is simply mentioned to generate the idea (of unity), but certainly there is no multiplicity."
>
> "The dualists affirm the birth of what is non-born. But how can what is non-born and immortal become mortal?"
>
> "The immortal can never become mortal, nor the mortal become immortal because there can be no change of nature."
>
> "It is on account of *māyā*—with the exclusion of every other possibility—that this Non-born may differentiate. If differentiation were real, then the immortal would become mortal."
>
> (III: 2, 15, 20, 21, 19)

According to Parmenides, opinion (*doxa* = representation, what appears to be true; sensory perception) is an erroneous vision of man 'in which true certainty does not dwell", and which makes Being seem to be generated and multiple. According to Gauḍapāda it is *avidyā*, which can also be taken to mean sensory perception (simple projection, opinion, mental representation), which makes appear things that are not.

---

1. The *Fragments* by Parmenides quoted here have been translated from Edizioni Laterza, Bari.

2. *Ibid.*

"Some researchers hold the birth of a thing already existing. Others, instead, hold the birth of what does not exist."

"A datum which already exists cannot be reborn and a datum which never existed cannot come into being."

"If a person believes that a positive, immortal entity can come into existence, how can he hold that the same immortal and unchangeable entity can yet maintain its immortal nature?"

"By the word nature is meant what is permanently acquired or is intrinsic or innate, what is not produced and what is unchanging in its essential characteristics."

"Cause [the fourth chapter of the *kārikās* deals with causation] cannot be born of an effect with no beginning; on the other hand an effect cannot be born of a cause without origin, because a thing without cause certainly has no birth."

"The unreal cannot have the unreal as its cause, nor can the real be born of the real, nor can the real stem from the unreal, nor, finally, the non-real from the real."

(IV: 3, 4, 8, 9, 23, 40)

5

ADVAITA VEDĀNTA

Q. We often hear people speak of *Advaita Vedānta* as religion, as philosophy, and metaphysics. But what is it really?

A. First of all we must underline the fact that certain questions are asked more in the West than in the East. In addition, the misunderstandings met with by many are worsened by the fact that some words have different meanings in the West and in the East.

It must also be pointed out that the answers given to the various questions are only meant as a stimulation towards a deepening of the knowledge to be acquired through the reading of specific and suitable texts.

In the West we have a concept of religion, philosophy and metaphysics that does not correspond to the Eastern meaning of the same terms. For us the concept of religion is derived from the Jewish-Christian-Islamic context and has a precise meaning connected with the theological constructions elaborated by those religions. To speak of Hindu religion may seem improper, because Hinduism, on the whole, and over the ages, more than an organized, hierarchical and dogmatic religion in the Western sense, is a 'way of being', of living, of expressing oneself. We may speak more appropriately of 'Hindu civilization', of 'Hindu consciousness', of 'Hindu attitude'.

Hinduism is based upon the *Vedas* which, rather than a theological or dogmatic *corpus* are a synthesis of philosophy, metaphysics, mysticism, cosmogony, traditional magic and other sciences and practices. The Hinduist would say that in the *Vedas* there is all that one needs to know. The seeds of the *Upaniṣadic* speculation and of the *Śāstras* are already present in the *Vedas*. The central ideas of Buddhism and of Jainism are not new. They, too, are present in the *Vedas*.

The Hinduist holds that the *Vedas*, and therefore the *Vedānta*, which are the later Scriptures that crown the *Vedas*, are *Sanātanadharma*, the eternal *dharma* above and beyond time. This *dharma*, being timeless, has no history because it has no beginning. Christianity, Judaism and Islamism can all be dated, they all have precise beginning and a founder: Jesus, Moses, Mohammed. Hinduism has no such founder. The *Ṛṣis* themselves, who drew up the *Vedas*, are only the transmitters of an eternal Truth which is non-human and beyond history. Many of the *Ṛṣis* are not even remembered by name; some of them have a name that is more mythical than real. For example, Vyāsa is held to be the compiler of the *Vedas*, of many other *Vedic* writings and of the very same *Mahābhārata*, but Vyāsa more than the name of a person refers to a 'function'. It is a mythical name and cannot be considered in the same way as the name Jesus or Moses.

In the West the concept of religion implies a founder (in space and time) who formulates certain moral-spiritual principles to be followed by the devotees. This is not so with Hinduism. To this concept of religion perhaps Buddhism is somewhat closer, but in this case, too, many distinctions must be made.

Therefore Hinduism is not a religion in the Western sense. It is also for this reason that it is not easy to accept or be part of or 'convert' to Hinduism. A Jew who wishes to become a Christian has only to be baptized to become automatically part of the Christian religious community, but for any person who wishes to become a Hindu it is not a question of being baptized, also because no such baptism exists. Some hold that one must be born a Hindu. But it is also true that in the West there are many 'Hindu consciousnesses' just as in the East many feel being Christians or Moslems. The term 'East' may be considered not in a geographical sense.

We should also note that in the East philosophy and religion go always together—the very opposite is true of modern West. In the East the one completes the other. Gauḍapāda, for instance, commented on the *Māṇḍūkya Upaniṣad* from the standpoint of the *Śruti* and of dialectical philosophy. In other words, he united *Revelation* and philosophical reflection.

With reference to the *Advaita Vedānta* it is not at all the case of speaking in terms of religion. The *Advaita Vedānta*—whose codifier was Śaṃkarācārya—is obviously linked to the *Vedas* of which it has grasped the purely philosophical and metaphysical factors. Its roots are, therefore, *Vedic.* The trunk was nourished by Gauḍapāda—the Teacher of Śaṃkara's Teacher—and the branched out tree with plenty of fruits was developed by Śaṃkara.

The *Advaita Vedānta* may be considered as philosophy and metaphysics, but these terms must not be taken in their Western sense.

In the West, especially in the modern West, philosophy is reserved to those who wish to 'demonstrate', through mental and discoursive dialectics, *their* own vision of the world and of Being. In other words, one tries to 'demonstrate' truth using discoursive reasoning, but we know that mental discourse has its limits because it can only operate on the plane of the objective and contingent. A rational, empirical 'demonstration' of Being, for example, implies setting oneself upon the plane of duality which, in turn, precludes not only the 'demonstration' itself but also the true *knowledge* of Being.

One may say that in the West philosophy suffers from the typically Western *consciential attitude* of looking at things from a dualistic, objective standpoint. It aims at knowing the external *object* while oriental thinking aims at knowing him who wants to know the external object.

Western philosophy is one of simple mental 'demonstration', Eastern philosophy is one of *realization.*

Besides, while the Western philosopher has produced a philosophical system of *his own,* often in contrast with and in opposition to the systems of other philosophers, the Eastern philosopher has not produced a system nor has he claimed ownership of his enunciations.

The *Advaita Vedānta* (like all other *darśanas*) is a *darśana* stemming from the *Vedas,* drawing from the *Vedas,* which develops a 'perspective' or 'point of view' that already existed in germ in the *Vedas.* The word *darśana,* in fact, is not indicative of a closed philosophical system thought by some solitary thinker-philosopher; its etymological meaning is 'to look', 'to observe', 'point of view' concerning the Vedic Scriptures, i.e. *Vedas* and *Upaniṣads* (*Śruti*). But even Greek philosophy, in its precise meaning, was a philosophy which derived its content from the *Mysteries*. The *Mysteries* are a branch of that eternal Doctrine which we have called *Sanātanadharma*. Orpheus, Pythagoras, Plato, Plotinus—to name but a few—all drew from the *Mysteries*. And Christianity, while availing of the *Sacred Mysteries* (in the Mass, in fact, the statement 'let us celebrate the Sacred Mysteries' is made) has refused and repudiated them. Thus, when we speak of philosophy we refer to that *Philosophia Perennis* which has no history and was not formulated by a human mind.

The term *metaphysics* has a more specific meaning and refers to that branch of philosophy which deals with the absolute Reality beyond all contingency, above the manifest in its integral extension, and, therefore, beyond time, space and cause.

In modern West whoever speaks of metaphysics... may be burnt at the stake. So strong is the negation of the transcendent today. But, in truth, in modern West not even philosophy exists any more, because it has been reduced to the level of philosophy of science, of politics, of law, etc.

6

METAPHYSICAL REALIZATION

Q. We often hear speaking of realization of the Self, of the *ātman*, of the Spirit, etc., but what is meant by metaphysical realization?

A. First of all let us see the etymological meaning of these terms or we may misunderstand each other.

What do we mean by realization? The verb 'to realize' means 'to make something become real', 'to translate into reality', 'to verify', to 'actuate', etc.

The meaning that is nearest to our case is 'to actuate'. 'To actuate' means, in fact, 'to pass from potentiality to act', 'to translate into *actuality* what is virtual'.

The term 'actuate' implies, therefore, something that already exists. On the other hand, we could not actuate or translate into effectuality what does not exist. Thus a child that grows actuates, realizes or manifests the physical and psychological potentialities that already exist in it. From this example we can understand that there is an *actuation* of even the psycho-physical qualities inherent in the individual. The majority of individuals do nothing but *realize* their own dreams, ideals, representation, those qualities peculiar to their own psychological and physical self.

If being in his totality were just individuality, empirical self, this kind of actuation would give him fulfilment and beatitude. However, we know that this is not so. Individuality is unhappy, dualistic, restless and dissatisfied; hence we have to admit that his own actuation is not sufficient, or else it is a *false actuation*.

The empirical materialist tries to realize-actuate himself as an ego-individuality, but the world of the ego is full of conflict and pain, and egoistical and sensory happiness is so fleeting that it cannot even be tasted.

Fortunately there is another kind of realization-actuation, that is inherent to the Self, to the true nature of the total being, to the spirit-*ātman*, to the Being as such, to the divine part in us, if you wish to use more comprehensible terms.

This kind of realization is the actuation of our true Essence. And in the actuation of one's own essence there cannot be conflict or bewilderment because it is a process which responds to the nature of the very same being; it is not an event contrary to nature. It is in the very nature of the Being.

In individuation there is conflict and suffering because the emphasis is placed not on the being-Essence, but on the *false representation* that one has of oneself. From this point of view the term realization can be replaced by another one: *liberation*. Liberation from what? Liberation from the *false representation* that we are a free, distinct and separate individuality, self-sufficient and divided from our being-Essence, from our true Ego which, to avoid confusion with the false ego, we call Self. Individuality does not actuate the true potentiality, but only its own projections which it produces artificially and which, as a consequence, are for ever changing. We—as individualities—pursue false ideals, false passions, false truths so that in the non-actuation of our true potentiality we experience conflict and are as if in blindness or ignorance (*avidyā*).

When, for instance, we see a snake instead of a rope—just to use the classical instance—all our actions and behaviour are in line with the snake 'reality'. But, in behaving so, it is obvious that we come up against conflict due to the fact that the snake is not the effective reality; it is not the true potentiality that we have to actuate and manifest. It is just a false representation of the rope that we have conjured up. On the other hand, in order to be in harmony with true and authentic realization, we must actuate the rope-*ātman*-Self which is the only absolute Reality and which, in itself, is beyond every process of potentiality and act.

Q. So there is freedom of the ego and freedom from the ego, is there not?

A. Yes, the ego-snake, in order to be able to gratify all sorts of insatiable desires, needs to be without impediments or to feel free to actuate all it wishes. And this is impossible due to the very nature of existence; but even if we conceded to the ego any kind of freedom, it would not be happy or fulfilled. Why? Because fulfilment is not in the *nature* of the ego, as this is only a false product or a false representation. What does not exist potentially cannot actuate or realize itself. Although the moon may wish to appropriate light from outside of itself, it will never become a sun. The human physical body, though it may live for any incredible length of time, will never become immortal because one cannot 'become' but *is* immortal; and if one *is*, one does not seek immortality.

The empirical ego, because *it is not*, has to find its fulfilment, its *raison d'être* and its realization *outside of itself*; and indeed it is obliged to, it needs to. This means that at best it may find some kind of gratification, but a gratification that comes from other than itself cannot be permanent bliss-fulfilment. If one is dependent and under the sway of the law of necessity one cannot be in harmony, pacified, blissful and fulfilled. If the empirical ego is searching, desiring and longing for, it means that it *is not* and every one of its realizations is a false realization, a false achievement.

Q. Therefore metaphysical realization is needed. What does this concept mean?

A. We have already spoken about realization and now we shall apply ourselves to understand the term *metaphysics*.

Originally the term metaphysics meant a series of texts which, on the basis of the order given to the Work of Aristotle, came after the texts called *Physics*. The subject treated by Aristotle in that Series of writings was called *Philosophia Prima*.

In time the term took on the meaning of 'beyond' matters belonging to the physical sphere, to become the 'science of the real in itself, seen as *beyond* immediate tangible appearance'.

From this point of view metaphysics has a position of superiority compared with the other fields of knowledge. Above all the various sciences of the *finite*, which deal with the partial, phenomenal and incomplete relations of being, there is the science of Reality in itself.

Metaphysics is the science of *aseity* (the property of a being which has in itself the reason and the end of its own existence), while physics is the science of *abaliety* (property of a being which finds the reason of its existence in other than itself).

We may also add that physics deals with the relative-contingent, which depends on other than itself, while metaphysics deals with what *is* or the Absolute and this rests on itself, with itself and for itself.

If we understand the term metaphysics then *metaphysical realization* means the achievement of the Absolute or of *aseity*.

Q. Can we go deeper into the concept of the Absolute?

A. According to the philosopher G. Zamboni, the term Absolute means: 'Etymologically that which is *free from relations,* or which exists and is what it is, without any need to be in relation with anything else, or what is fully sufficient, self-sufficient, independently of any other thing or reality.... Therefore the Totality of the real, the Real as a whole, must be self-sufficient, fully independent to exist or to be what it is.... With the concept of being or entity or reality the idea of totality is formed: 'all that exists', 'all Reality', 'the whole of Reality', outside of which there is nothing. The 'whole of Reality' cannot depend on something else outside of itself, because outside of it there is a mere nothing; thus the totality of what exists has in itself full sufficiency to exist and full independence. Either the 'totality of Reality' is itself the Absolute and the Independent or else It contains them. In any case the Absolute exists; one cannot doubt it; if anything, the existence of the insufficient and the dependent and its relation with the Absolute is less clear. But certainly, if there is something that exists, the Absolute exists.' (*Dizionario Filosofico*, Milano 1978)

Metaphysical realization therefore aims at the *actuation* of what is 'free from relations', of what has 'no need to be in relation with anything else', because it is *aseity*. Let us see what Gauḍapāda says in his *kārikās* to the *Māṇḍūkya Upaniṣad* (IV, 2 and III, 39):

> 'I bow to this *yoga*—taught by the Scriptures—well known as *asparśa*, free from relations, beneficial, generator of

> beatitude for all beings, free from oppositions and contradictions....'
>
> 'This *yoga* which is called *asparśa* (without contact or relation) is difficult to understand for many *yogins* because they, feeling fear where there is none, are afraid of it.'[1]

And Śaṃkara comments: "*Asparśa* is the *yoga* without *sparśa*: contact or connection with anything at all; it is of the very nature of *Brahman* [Absolute]. Those who know *Brahman* call it by this name; in other words *Asparśa-yoga* is that which is free from all relation. It becomes a blessing for all beings.... We can say that the enjoyment of any particular type of object may bring happiness, but not constant well-being [we stated above that the happiness of the empirical ego is always contingent and fleeting because it is based on external factors]; this *yoga*, instead, brings blessings and at the same time stable well-being because its nature is beyond the non-permanent. Besides it is devoid of opposition. Why? Because it is devoid of contradictions [individuality is based on opposition because it expresses itself upon the ego-non ego plane].... The idea is that this truth can only be realized as consequence of an impetus the crowning of which is awareness of the *ātman* as sole Reality.... The non-discriminating fear, while practising this *yoga*, the extinction of their individuality, although (*asparśa*) is beyond all fear.

Those who believe the mind and the sense organs to be the snake superimposed on the rope, therefore having no reality independent of *Brahman*, identify with *Brahman* without fear enjoying in a natural way that eternal peace, called emancipation, which depends on no other factor."

Those who think that the psychological or empirical ego is their true reality undoubtedly fear metaphysical realization because they believe they will extinguish, annihilate and lose themselves. And wanting at all costs to avoid the death of their ego—which is in any case perishable—they invent

1. *Ibid.*

philosophies and sciences to support and satisfy their insecurity and incompleteness.

This philosophical vision is typical of the present day where the mirage and illusion of the 'golden calf' appears as the solution to the 'well-being' of the ego.

Q. So *Asparśa* realization has no other aim than to *actuate oneself* in metaphysical Unity?

A. The dualist philosophy cannot lead to the realization of metaphysical Unity. At most it can achieve a mathematical unity which implies duality and which is not the Absolute.

On the contrary, true metaphysical realization implies actuating our most profound nature which is Non-duality. Now, our true nature (not that illusory 'second nature' represented by our empirical ego) is achieved by an act of Knowledge and of Identity.

To disclose our true nature we do not need any particular physical or mental 'exercise', though they may be used at the preparatory stages, but we have to eliminate the qualitative *superimpositions* that have been projected upon the Self-Being.

Q. Is metaphysical realization a question of knowledge, then?

A. This question helps to clarify further the concept of 'actuation' or of 'potentiality' and 'act'.

Metaphysical Unity is pure actuation and excludes all passages from potentiality to act: to speak of the eternally present and infinite Being in terms of even theoretical phases is impossible. The Ever Present has no history, it has no actuation, it has no movement because it has no generation (*ajāti*). Metaphysical realization, rather than a question of actuation-realization as presented above, is an act of immediate knowledge and awareness, because pure Being is not attained by steps or through supports, nor can pure Being be grasped in the process actuation.

If we fail to understand, through intellection, what we are and what we are not we shall always remain in the sphere of sensory perception and of subject-object otherness.

Q. However, many kinds of *yoga* and religious doctrines adopt empirical media rather than Knowledge.

A. Most people, by means of empirical media, 'actuate' *samādhis* which imply simple experimentation of individual states of consciousness, states outside of the dense and gross sphere.

Individuality is not confined to the corporeal state, but extends also into the subtle, though substantial, one. However, in the subtle and even in the causal state (the three levels of existential manifestation) we are not in the realm of the Absolute or in the metaphysical sphere.

Pure Being is attained through Being, through a consciousness awakening which resolves itself in Identity or in *being* Being.

7

THE THREE STATES OF BEING

Q. What do the three states of Being and the Fourth, mentioned in the *Māṇḍūkya Upaniṣad*, mean? There is also mention of the three worlds of manifestation; do these correspond to the three states? Some speak of seven worlds; is this perhaps in disagreement with the teaching of the *Upaniṣads*?

A. Every world can be subdivided into other worlds or spheres of existence; therefore mention is made of three, five, seven and even ten worlds. The number is of little importance. It depends upon the point of view from which one wishes to examine things. For example, the physical plane may be taken as a whole or divided into its solid, liquid and gaseous dimensions; we know that, within each of these live and move entities which are different from one another. Thus in the 'liquid' dimension, although it belongs to the gross-physical domain, a world quite apart from the solid one lives and moves and may even be considered as a world unto itself with its own specific qualities. In any case, we can say with the *Upaniṣad*:

> "All this is surely *Brahman*. This *ātman* is *Brahman* and *ātman* has four quarters (*pāda*).
>
> "The first quarter (*pāda*) is *vaiśvānara*, whose sphere (of action) is the waking state....
>
> "The second quarter (*pāda*) is *taijasa* (the luminous), whose sphere of action is the state of dreaming....
>
> "The third quarter (*pāda*) is *prājña*, whose sphere of action is deep sleep....
>
> "The Sages believe that the Fourth.... is invisible, non-acting...."
>
> (*Māṇḍūkya Upaniṣad*: II, III, IV, V, VII)

The *Māṇḍūkya* is defined as that *Upaniṣad* which alone synthesizes the whole of *Vedānta* teaching. We find in it the enunciation of the three states of Being as well as the Fourth which refers to the metaphysical and transcendent state.

All branches, both Western and Eastern, of the Tradition recognize the fact that the one Being expresses Itself, on the plane of manifestation, in different vital states, in different existential forms or in various modes. One may also say that Being expresses Itself in various vibratory states of consciousness, both at the formal and formless levels. It follows that we have to distinguish the existential plane from the entities that live and are in it. Let us take, as an instance, the dense physical plane, that is, the plane on which we are experiencing our present lives. It is a plane of existence. It is formed by solid, liquid and gaseous vibrations, etc., which belong to the gross plane of *vaiśvānara*; in all these vibratory states, as we already mentioned, there are entities that live, move and exist. In the liquid state of the ocean there is an entire world, a way of being, millions of entities that express their qualities through well-defined forms; in the gaseous state, or in the air, as many millions more of entities carry on their existence and their being, and so on.

When the *Upaniṣad* speaks of *vaiśvānara* it refers to our bodily state, our physical being, our gross state, which corresponds to the gross universal plane of Being (*Virāṭ*). Therefore we have that *viśva*, or the entity identified with *viśva*, experiments upon a portion of the *Virāṭ* plane.

Viśva is the individual entity, *Virāṭ* is the universal Entity, therefore *Virāṭ* is not only our planet but the totality of the worlds that express themselves upon the gross plane.

The sphere of action, of manifestation of the *jīva-viśva* (the soul embodied upon the gross plane) is that which man normally calls, waking--naturally as compared with dream and sleep. Through this state of consciousness and upon the existential plane of *Virāṭ*, the human *jīva* has various kinds of experience. This state is characterized by *ahaṃkāra* (the sense of ego), by *manas* (the empirical projective mind), by *kāma* (desire in its indefinite expressions) and by the gross physical body (*sthūlaśarīra* or *annamayakośa*, body made of food). Therefore the *jīva,* by means of appropriate *bodies* of manifestation, with their respective senses and faculties, experiences the *vaiśvānara* sphere.

The world of the bodies-*viśva* is a world of needs, tension and conflict because it is essentially a world of want, poverty and non-being.

But, besides the dense physical plane, the *jīva*-entity experiences with its subtle body (*liṅgaśarīra*) another existential plane, that of *Hiraṇyagarbha.*

Hiraṇyagarbha is a plane, a vibratory state or an existential condition even more extensive than the state of *Virāṭ.* We do not perceive it with our physical senses because these are only capable of perceiving the *Virāṭ* sphere. When the *jīva*-entity leaves its gross body—due to illness or other reasons—it moves on to the state of *taijasa* which is luminous; luminous because it illumines itself. Thus, dreams are illumined by our own light.

The *taijasa*-entity with its vehicle made of more subtle and vibrating matter, having, like the dense physical vehicle, *instruments* of contact—senses and faculties—experiences life inherent in the universal plane of *Hiraṇyagarbha.* During physical embodiment, these senses and faculties belonging to the subtle body are dormant, although some are able to develop them; in this case we speak of extrasensory perception.

The sphere of *Hiraṇyagarbha*—as the *Virāṭ* one—has many 'environmental levels' where the *jīva*-entities with their luminous bodies find opportunities of manifestation. Particularly on the subtle level what guides the *jīva* towards one or the other dimension is its vibratory state, its 'qualities', its energetic patrimony that it has qualified in a certain way. Thus we speak of *kāmaloka, mānavaloka* or of *Hiraṇyaloka. Kāmaloka* (*loka*: place in the sense of state) is the 'environmental level' characterized by the quality of desire-sentiment in all its expressive range. *Mānavaloka* is the 'environmental level' characterized by the more creative, mental, ideal qualities, though still under the sway of *ahaṃkāra*, the sense of ego or the individualized state.

Hiraṇyaloka is the 'environmental level' no longer characterized by individualized qualities but by universal ones. It is the sphere of archetypes, or 'Ideas' that do not belong to the ego, whose sphere is *mānavaloka*, but to the universal Being. The soul (*jīva*) upon its true plane 'contemplates' not its own ideal reflections, but 'Ideas'.

Where do the highest expressions of Genius come from? They come from the sphere of *Hiraṇyaloka*. One may say that the Soul has found its 'homeland' at last, its 'place', its 'home'. The *kāma*-desire and the *manas*-empirical mind are no longer needed upon the *Hiraṇyaloka* level; the Soul *sees, contemplates* and immediately comprehends. Here, to see means to know (*veda* in Sanskrit derives from the root *vid* which means to see-know).

The *kāma*-desire, being an expression of 'want', of 'lacking' (not being and not possessing the ego desires), has no cause to exist as the Soul, upon its own plane, *is*.

In dreams everything comes to us. In dreams we are not in need of anything. We only have to project all we desire within our particular sphere of existence.

But *Hiraṇyaloka, mānavaloka*, etc., are not dreams as such. They are equated to dream only because they are analogous to them, and analogy is not identity.

Noetic life is fullness of *action*; in that it is a reflection of the *ātman*, it possesses the consciousness of *sat, cit, ānanda*.

> "This is the life of the gods, without sorrow and blessed; evil is nowhere here, and if things had stopped here there would not have been any evil, only a first and the second and third goods."
>
> (*Enneads*: I, 8, ii)

Prājña is the germinal, causal state, that is, the state from which the determinations of manifestation arise. It is the geometrical point which, while having no dimension, is the origin of the line and the plane. It is the noumenon, it is a germ containing being in all its potentiality.

The entity-*jīva-prājña* manifests itself upon the existential level of Being, of *Īśvara*; this is the *Brahmaloka* level, the abode of Brahmā, where multiplicity dissolves into unity.

In it we can see how the three states are but one having different modes of expression; in it there are no distinctions, there is no duality, there is no opposition. He who discovers this condition has the privilege of *seeing* the unity of life, of understanding how consciousness has become so vast as to embrace the whole of existence. The entities and the planes are not without but within oneself, because there is no without and therefore no within. Oneness *is*, and it is everywhere in its indivisibility.

Prājña is assimilated to deep dreamless sleep, because in *prājña* everything goes back to silence, to non-becoming, to non-motion. Therefore, waking, dreaming and deep dreamless sleep correspond to *vaiśvānara, taijasa* and *prājña*, and as waking, dreaming and deep sleep are experienced by a sole witness, so *vaiśvānara*, the gross state, *taijasa*, the subtle state and *prājña*, the germinal state, are all experienced by one and the same witness (*sākṣin*), the only real and constant factor, while the three states appear and disappear. This witness, also called *avasthātrayasākṣin* (witness of the three states) is a reflection, on the plane of the manifest, of the transcendent *Brahman-ātman* (the Fourth) beyond the three states, while at the same time permeating them.

Q. Have these states a correspondence with other traditional Branches?

A. Yes, according to the Mysterical Tradition, synthesized by Plotinus, we have three states or dimensions which represent the realm of the formal and non-formal manifestation, as well as a fourth called the metaphysical One, which is beyond the Spirit-Being itself.

In the *Corpus Hermeticum* (X, 14) it is said:

> "All things depend upon a sole principle, and this principle depends on the One and only [that is, on the One without a second of the *Vedānta* Tradition]. While the principle is in movement in order to become the principle again, the One and only stands still and is not subject to movement."

8

MĀYĀ

Q. What is meant by the term *māyā*?

A. The term has a number of different meanings according to the points of view of the different *Vedāntic* currents. Thus, phenomenon, *prakṛti*-nature, *śakti, avidyā,* that which renders possible the impossible, taking one thing for another, veiling superimposition, etc. refer all to *māyā.*

Q. What is meant, for example, by 'veiling superimposition'?

A. It means superimposing a thing upon another thus taking a thing to be something else. For example, we can superimpose the colour blue upon the sky which is really colourless. We can superimpose the physical body upon the pure *ātman* so that we fall into the error of considering the physical body as being absolute and real. We can superimpose a 'concept' upon a reality, the nature of which is different. In this way we had, for a long time, a 'concept' of matter which we have to rectify. This implies that we superimposed an erroneous idea upon the datum called 'matter'.

Superimposition is caused by two factors: the one projective —we *project* with our imagination an idea, a concept, etc.—, the other veiling, because the projection veils and hides the reality of the datum. In fact, the blue colour that we have projected upon the sky hides the true nature of the sky, just as the concept of physical body, which we have projected upon the *ātman*, hides as a result the true nature of the *ātman.*

Māyā is not a real-absolute datum, it does not belong to the category of tangible objects, it can be recognized by simple ascertainment. For example, we might easily take a piece of rope—if we saw it lying in a country lane—to be a snake; in this case we have superimposed the concept of 'snake', or the image-snake, upon the rope, which is not the snake. But on looking more carefully we recognize, or ascertain, that the snake does not exist and what really exists is instead a rope. Who fooled us? *Māyā.* From this standpoint we can say that the 'projection' of the snake is the outcome of an error of perception, the effect of not knowing, the fruit of *avidyā* (ignorance concerning the true *nature* of a thing).

Q. What is meant by saying that *māyā* is synonymous with *prakṛti*-nature?

A. *Prakṛti* is the equivalent of *natura naturans,* of substance, of 'matter' (in a special sense), of the universal Mother that produces bodies, forms of all dimensions and degrees.

It is the plastic and eternal substance (as a pole of the essence) from which all things produced are made. A body-form (such as a cloud in the sky or a mineral or vegetal body) which is born, grows and dies represents a phenomena; therefore, *māyā-prakṛti* is a producer of phenomena. All we see around us is phenomenon, it is *māyā-prakṛti.*

This *prakṛti*-matter—as we now know—not only undergoes endless change, but can resolve itself into other grades of energetic density; mass can resolve itself into energy and physical energy into subtle, superphysical energy, or into non-matter. All bodies and planes of existence are made of *māyā-prakṛti* stuff. Therefore, *māyā* is synonymous with *prakṛti,* with phenomenon, with movement-change, since a body is the result of a particular *māyika movement.*

Śakti is the name given to nature in movement.

Q. We are all *māyā-śakti* then?

A. If the human individual were made of only the physical body we would be obliged to give a positive answer. The dense physical body of man is *māyā,* because it is matter, phenomenon, movement-change. It is born, it grows and dies; it is subject therefore to transformation, change, dissolution. This is the conception of the materialist who considers matter to be the absolute reality.

But for the traditional Philosophy, man is not merely *māyā-prakṛti,* he is also *puruṣa,* that is *ātman,* Spirit, Essence or Being. We therefore have the polarity *puruṣa-prakṛti*; we have Being which through quantity-substance expresses qualities. When the *puruṣa* withdraws from its manifest body, this remains inert, void of intelligence, of will and of self-consciousness. Intelligence and will, like self-consciousness, are consubstantial aspects of the *puruṣa*, while *prakṛti-māyā*-substance is only 'sentient'. *Puruṣa* can detach itself from its physical body and perceive clearly how its material *instrument* is something other than itself. Moreover, it can be aware, in an intelligent way, of being able to operate, manifest and express itself on other existential levels beyond the dense physical one.

Q. What does the physical body represent, then, for the *puruṣa-essence*?

A. A body, at whatever dimension or level it may be, is an instrument of contact and of expression capable of operating upon an existential level of life. To live and operate upon the dense physical plane, for example, we must have a body of expression or an instrument capable of establishing relations with that existential plane. However, the body is only an instrument of contact which can be taken up or dropped.

Q. Is man therefore made of the dualism of being and non-being, essence and substance?

A. Earlier we talked of *polarity* which resolves itself into a transcendental point, a metaphysical point where polarity or what we conceptually call being and non-being disappears.

Q. If also *māyā-prakṛti* is a polarity of the metaphysical Point, why are we told that *māyā-prakṛti* must be rejected?

A. The metaphysics of Non-duality does not say to desert, reject or negate *māyā*. Such an attitude belongs to the sphere of *avidyā*. What *Asparśa* metaphysics tells us is not to create identification or identify with *māyā*, not to superimpose *māyā* upon *puruṣa* or the metaphysical Point, taking—as in the classical example—the rope for the snake.

If we believe ourselves to be exclusively body-vehicle-form (therefore *prakṛti*) we fall into *avidyā*, that is, we fall into the error of considering as absolute that which is not absolute or to consider that which is *imperishable-constant* as changeable and perishable. The disharmony, aberration and chaos of the human individuality derive from the fact that the individual considers himself to be only body-form, therefore limitation, since each body represents a limitation-bondage of being.

Q. Can *avidyā* be considered absolute, real and permanent?

A. If it were real-absolute we could never eliminate it. Therefore we would be obliged to remain in incompleteness-ignorance; we would always remain in error without any hope of escape.

Q. And where does *avidyā* go when it is dispelled?

A. It comes from nowhere and it goes nowhere. When we discover that the rope is not a snake, where does the error go? Or else, when we wake up where does the world of dreams, projected upon the screen of our 'aura' and made of the stuff of *prakṛti*-substance, go?

When we manifest an idea, a thought, we shape a definite and geometrical mental image that an acute clairvoyant can see.

Now, when we stop thinking, where does the form-image go? This entire phenomenal universe is an *idea* materialized by *Mahat* (universal Mind) and, when the supreme *puruṣa* stops 'imagining', it vanishes like a cloud in the sky.

We have to eliminate two types of identification or of superimposition which are the product of *avidyā*, but which are two moments of the same process: one is when we believe ourselves to be image-form-body, the other is when we believe ourselves to be *prakṛti* at the non-formal or undifferentiated stage. We, as *puruṣa*, and more so as metaphysical Point, are beyond the world of names and forms, beyond *prakṛti*-substance itself.

Prakṛti is the instrumental cause of the world of names and forms. It is the stuff the individual and the universal 'dreams' are made of, while *puruṣa* is the first cause of the movement of *prakṛti*.

The profound recognition of what we really are is the goal of Śaṃkara's *Advaita* and Gauḍapāda's *Asparśavāda*.

Conflict, disharmony and pain come to an end only with the

recognition of one's own identity. A society of individuals who do not acknowledge their most profound and elementary reality, is destined to live in alienation and conflict, notwithstanding all the philosophical, socio-political and sentimental formulae it can 'create' in time-space; time-space represents another name for *māyā*.

Q. Can *māyā*, therefore, solve the eternal problem of being and non-being, of ego and non-ego, and provide an answer to the question of how the Absolute has fallen into the relative?

A. Yes. Every duality (like real and non-real, being and non-being, ego and non-ego, absolute and relative, etc.) is the outcome of mental representation, it is not real-absolute, it is not *aseity*.

Between Being and what we believe non-being to be exists *māyā*; it is sufficient to eliminate it to discover that only the absolute Being exists.

Between the rope and the snake or between the dreaming entity and the dream, there is *māyā*; it is sufficient to eliminate it to discover that only the rope or the dreaming entity exists.

The Absolute, if it is such, cannot fall into the relative or transform itself into the relative, as the absolute Good, if it is such, cannot become evil or anything else. What changes is not Reality in itself, but our *māyā* perspective of Reality. The rope remains a rope, but what changes (movement) is our perspective, our vision of the snake, of the trickle of water, of a stick, etc., which we superimpose upon the rope, etc.

Q. Can *māyā* be considered pure illusion?

A. *Māyā* is not an illusion in the Western sense of the word. An illusion produces nothing, it is non-existent; an illusory event can be compared to a hare's horns. Śaṃkara holds that the *māyika* universe is not like the hare's horns or the barren woman's child. In Western terms we can say that *māyā* is synonymous with phenomenon, with 'shaping and shaped movement'.

9

EXPERIENCER AND EXPERIENCED OBJECT

Q. What are the experiencer and the experienced object? Is there something besides this duality? What can they mean from a metaphysical point of view?

A. By looking at man's behaviour one can infer that his movements and decisions are characterized by the *experimentation* factor. It is commonly accepted that the individual is here on this plane of life to feel and experience 'sensations'. Even some spiritualist currents propose 'experience' as the aim and purpose of spirituality, holding that experience produces knowledge and realization.

We should therefore conclude, on the basis of this concept, that the human being determines himself, develops, knows, etc., through experience.

Experience as such is the result of a movement of qualities (*guṇas*) requiring expression. Feeling, desire, instinct, self-assertion, creative energy, etc., are human qualities that lead to experience. These qualities, when expressed and manifested, improve the individual's *faculties*, develop his specific crafts, thereby broadening his sphere of action.

But who is making experience? Who *needs* to make experience?

Experience requires an object to be experienced, a quality that tends to express itself, to create activity or to experience and a subject that is the enjoyer of the experience. Who then is the experiencer?

In psychological terms we may answer that this is the 'ego'. The ego seeks experience through qualities to be expressed, so as to feel gratified and complete.

When we fulfill a desire, expressed through a quality, the ego enjoys it, but it may not feel satisfied and may even feel frustrated if the *object* of its desire is removed or no longer present. This means that experience is not always pleasant or gratifying.

Someone may well advance the hypothesis that such a dual condition of frustration and gratification (in other words, pleasure-pain) might represent the ego's growth factor. At this point we should try to better understand what this ego, in search of experience, of gratification-frustration, or experiencing dualism, is.

All traditional branches consider being, in its totality, as made of three aspects: Spirit, soul and body. In *Vedāntic* terms these three are called *ātman, jīva* and *sthūla.* Which is, then, the aspect of being that seeks experiences or gratification-frustration?

The *ātman* or pure Spirit, being the Absolute in us, cannot seek experience because it is not subject to the law of *necessity.* The complete-in-itself cannot be in need of anything. The sun does not need or desire light seeing that it is itself light. In the same way, the knower cannot desire knowledge if he himself is knowledge.

Therefore, the experiencer cannot be the pure Spirit, the *ātman.* In order to find the experiencer we have to go below the level of the Spirit and on to other existential levels, where the Soul or the *jīvātman* manifests itself.

The Soul—the Spirit's reflection of consciousness, or a ray of the *ātman's* fire—expresses itself on three existential levels: the one called gross, the one called subtle or universal and the principial-noetic one. These are the three levels of manifestation mentioned by all branches of tradition.

The Soul, on the upper subtle and principial plane does not experience sensorially but is 'contemplation', while the *ahaṃkāra*, or the 'sense of ego', having fallen and finding itself on the lower subtle and gross planes (lower *taijasa* and *viśva*), acts, is spurred to produce, to create activity, to move outside of itself so as to be able to make experience.

We should now make a distinction between the 'action-without-action' of which the *Gītā* speaks, and simple doing or the promotion of interested and finalized activism; and according to the Western Mysteric Tradition, between *theōria* and *poiēsis*.

Pure *theōria* does not produce movement, and it does not even produce experience, it is not *necessity*. Pure *theōria*, which is contemplation—to be taken in its true meaning—is only a response of the being to life. Contemplation—in the meaning given to it by traditional Philosophy—is characterized by the *sattva* quality, or harmony. It is not desire, quest, acquisition, it is not motivated by physical or psychological interest. Contemplation is pure will, it is actuation; in actuation Being reveals itself without any dual psychological motivation; Being *is*, the act *is*.

Sensory action is, on the contrary, peculiar to the *ahaṃkāra*, to the empirical self which, living under the law of necessity and 'corruption', *must* do, *must* act, *must* move, projecting itself endlessly in the object.

Sensorial action is permeated with *rajas*. Activity brought to an extreme becomes *activism*, action for action's sake, action because one cannot stand still. Action leads to agitation, it is translatory movement in the direction of the object to be acquired, while contemplation is a rotating movement around one's own axis.

In pure action-actuation we have non-action or non-doing as it is a simple unveiling of being, while in emotional activity the being forgets and loses itself in the experienced event or in the object of experience. In empirical activity there is effort, oblivion of one's own true nature, there is becoming, there is time-space. Doing-agitation belongs to the empirical self, pure action is an *act* of the soul. Doing implies loss of the 'noumenality' of being and action-without-action is pure noetic act.

All empirical experiences are non-realities, they are *saṃsāra*; only That which is behind the experience and the experiencer is the ultimate Reality.

Pure action for the East is *līlā*, for the West, as we have seen, is *theōria*.

> "Contemplation, in its universal meaning, is the act by which each being takes up its place within the hierarchy of the

cosmos, attaining its own nature from the illuminated presence of the beings that come before it and propagating its reflections around itself to develop the beings that come after it. Contemplation, in fact, is an 'act unto itself', beyond any exterior or passionate impulse."

(P. Prini: *Plotino.* Abete-Roma)

".... So this must be something where both are really one. But this is living contemplation, not an object of contemplation like that in something else. For that which is in something else is alive because of the other, not in its own right."

(*Enneads*: III, 8, viii)

For Plotinus contemplation is being and actuation all at once, it is *theōria* and *poiēsis* transposed on to intelligible planes. It is necessary, however, to point out that experience, motivated by psychological doing, cannot lead to Being but goes on endlessly on the plane of becoming. It can improve certain faculties, it can sharpen astuteness, it can lead to *manasic* or mental development, it can give 'power', but it cannot grant freedom, nor fulfilment, nor enlightenment, nor contemplation.

"Two lovely birds, inseparable friends, live together on the same tree. One feeds upon the sweet fruit of the *pippala*, the other without eating looks on."

(*Muṇḍaka Upaniṣad*: III, 1)

".... Now the soul which comes from the divine was quiet, standing in itself according to its character; but the body, in a tumult because of its weakness, flowing away itself and battered by the blows from outside, first cried out to the community of the living thing and imparted its disturbance to the whole."

(*Enneads*: VI, 4, xv)

One is the *jīva* or individual spirit, characterized by action, by doing, by acquiring and experiencing the fruits of pleasure-pain; the other is the motionless *ātman* characterized by *Pax profunda*, by being what it is.

10

THE FALL OF THE SOUL

Q. Empirical science holds that man comes from below, developing through a series of transformations and evolutionary processes spread out over time.

The Sacred Science, on the other hand holds that man comes from above and that if he is now in this world of conflict this is due to the so-called 'fall'.

How can we solve this problem?

A. The problem is certainly challenging and by no means easy to solve if one wishes to examine it using only simple sensory instruments. Is man the outcome of 'evolution' or of 'involution'? Is he the product of Being or of becoming?

Again, if man is composed of spirit-*noûs*, soul-*psyché* and body-*sôma*, to which of these elements must we attribute the evolutionary process?

Scientific empiricism defines man as a system of organs that produce intelligence, will, perception and consciousness. In other words, for this scientific philosophy man, being a body, a form, a complex cannot but undergo mutation and development. The human physical structure of the Paleolithical era is not identical with that of the present day.

The Sacred Science has nothing to argue against this point. Every form is change, process and becoming. But the being is not merely *sôma*-body-cell, it is also *noûs*, it is also *psyché*, to use terms belonging to the Western Tradition; it is also Soul, which pre-exists the body and therefore survives after the dissolution of the body.

Parapsychology and even a number of psychological currents are interested in factors that go beyond the physical level. So the problem may be seen from a different angle: does the *noûs*, the Spirit, the *ātman*, or in other words, Being evolve?

The question being this, the problem of evolution or involution proposes the theme of Being and becoming or non-being.

What is it that becomes, and what is it that does not?

Elsewhere we examined the problem of Being and non-being and we also considered the question of the impossibility for Being or pure Spirit to evolve.[1]

Here we may consider the concept of fall. In fact, Tradition speaks of the Soul's fall, which implies that the Soul comes from Above. But what is meant by fall? And who has fallen?

It is held by some that man is a 'stunned God', by others that he is a 'fallen Angel'—which is really the same thing. Others hold that man, having disobeyed his Creator, has been banished to a world of conflict, and others still that, as he had freedom of choice, he has tied himself down with his own hands. There are other points of view, but we can draw some conclusions.

The fall, from a philosophical point of view rather than a mystical one, may be taken to mean the scission of something that was once whole and integral. This split may produce oblivion of one's original oneness, thus generating duality. Unity is divided and the being, no longer a synthesis, is compelled to wander (movement) until it once more finds its unity. The one has fallen into the two, therefore into multiplicity, and in multiplicity there can be no synthesis and no homogeneousness, that is, no completeness. The scission is an act of alienation.[2]

If a human being, at a purely psychological level, were to be divided, his case would become pathological because, by losing his original individual identity, he would be forced to live in uncertainty and bewilderment. We can say that such a person would live like a ghost, a sleeper, or a sleep-walker. Likewise the individual, by dividing himself, has identified with his phenomenon-ghost, with his instruments of contact, with his vehicles or bodies of manifestation, forgetting his other, we may say, divine counterpart. Some say that man has two selves, his divine Self and his individual one.

---

1. Cp. especially the chapter *Ajātivāda* and *Asparśavāda* in this book.

2. Cp. Raphael's *La Filosofia dell'Essere,* last chapter. Edizioni Āśram Vidyā. Roma, 1978.

Restless, constantly on the move, violent and troubled, man is in search of his forgotten *half*; he is in search of his own oneness and completeness. His restlessness is legitimate. What is not legitimate is the direction that it takes.

The human being, although for ever seeking for his other half outside himself in the world of objects, will never be happy. However much he may give vent to his restlessness by acquiring material wealth, by self-asserting, in the quest for power, in wars, sex, family, etc., he will never be happy. He may dull himself, he may lose himself indefinitely in objects of all kinds, but he will never be happy and in peace, because he is without his other half. This is a fact and an evidence that needs no demonstration. Until he becomes *reintegrated*, even if he becomes master of the whole world, he cannot be happy and serene. He will always feel incomplete, unfulfilled, dissatisfied and will undoubtedly be missing something else. This urge to *search* is so strong because oneness—never truly extinguished in the individual—demands oneness. Every human desire is indicative of something missing, and however much man may comply with it, he will never feel satisfied until and unless such a desire is turned into an aspiration for unity.

Desire is restlessness, is psychological movement; it is a burning need for satisfaction in order to gratify the maimed half that thirsts for completeness. Desire comes from scission and can be resolved only by putting the two halves together again.

From what has been said we can deduce that the demagogues to be feared most are those who try to offer up the 'things' of this phenomenal-material world to the mutilated part of being, to this half of the individual, which is eagerly looking for its happiness or its completeness, making him believe that they represent the solution to his problem. It is the vision of the 'golden calf'. In modern times this scission has widened and, as a consequence, the thirst for 'things' has grown.

Q. If the pure *ātman*-spirit can never fall into duality, who has divided then?

A. All the traditional Branches agree in maintaining that the scission concerns the Soul, or *jīvātman* or *psyché* which is a reflection of the pure Spirit. Just as the individual in a dream, who experiences duality, is a projection of the mind, so too the Soul is a simple projection of *ātman*.

Q. How does the scission occur?

A. This 'projection' or reflection of the *ātman* attracts towards itself 'matter' from the various planes of existence and makes vehicles or bodies of manifestation from it; then it *identifies* with these bodies forgetting its true origin. The myth of Narcissus explains this phenomenon and this process very well. We can understand all this only through images and analogies.

Q. Is the individual, a shadow of *ātman*, obliged to identify with its other 'shadow'?

A. He is not obliged, but he is free to do so.

Q. Can you give me an example by way of illustration?

A. In our mind we can conjure up an ideal, a passion, etc., and identify with it to such an extent as to forget that we are individuals above and beyond passions and ideas. We can dream while wide awake (and wakefulness is also a dream) and identify with our dreams to such a degree that we lose our identity. This happens to the majority of people; in fact, they are not persons but teachers, politicians, tradesmen, fathers, mothers, children, etc.; they are everything and anything but entities aware of their true and profound reality.

When we become one with what we are not or with 'things'—and even our bodies, an ideal and an emotion are things—the scission has taken place. When we have become 'thing' ourselves, we have lost our identity and our freedom. We may even say that by identifying with an object we have 'fallen', that we are no longer ourselves apart from being number-quality. "Oblivion is therefore his wickedness." (*Corpus Hermeticum*: X, 15)

Q. Can the individual then avoid creating the scission?

A. We have said that he may or may not do so, this depends upon his *freedom* to be, which is inherent in his nature.

However, we should remember that Being is by nature an indivisible unity that cannot split or become two. Thus it is obvious that the scission (word which undoubtedly is inadequate to express the concept we wish to propose) is not in an absolute sense a loss of balance in the unity, but the nature of Being is such that it can manifest an unlimited number of expressions. The fall or the scission must not be considered as becoming other than Being, but as representing a *mode* of being. A piece of ice is an expression and a mode of water, but one cannot say that an absolute scission or an irreversible fall has occurred in water. Human experience is a 'mode of being', a state of consciousness of Being.

Q. Therefore the fall is not an act of divine will.

A. No. Man is divided because he wants to. He is passionate because he so desires. He is born upon this plane of existence because he so desires, man is even an individual because he so desires.

Q. Therefore the Tradition is simply pointing to the solution of this scission.

A. Yes. The Tradition is the depositary of this fundamental truth. It teaches the restless, conflicting individual how he can find the way back to unity. Traditional symbology refers to this process of scission and its consequent recomposition; this is the symbology of Isis and Osiris in ancient Egypt and of Orphism in Greece. In other words, it is the symbology of the Sacred Mysteries of the West as well as that of the *Veda-Upaniṣads*.

The death and rebirth of the initiations are nothing more than a profound symbol. It is necessary to die to what one is not in order to be reborn to what one really is.

While the philosophy of becoming perpetuates the state of scission and conflict, the Philosophy of being resolves it by bringing the being back to Being.

> "What is it, then, which has made the souls forget their father, God, and be ignorant of themselves and Him, even though they are parts which come from His higher world and

altogether belong to it? The beginning of evil for them was audacity and coming to birth and the first otherness and the wishing to belong to themselves. Since they were clearly delighted with their own independence, and made great use of self-movement, running the opposite course and getting as far away as possible, they were ignorant even that they themselves came from that world, just as children who are immediately torn from their parents and brought up far away do not know who they themselves or their parents are. Since they do not any more see their father or themselves, they despise themselves through ignorance of their birth and honour other things, admiring everything rather than themselves and, astonished and delighted at and dependent on these [earthly] things, they broke themselves loose as far as they could in contempt of that from which they turned away. So their honour for these things here and their contempt for themselves are the causes of their utter ignorance of God. For what pursues and admires something else admits at the same time its own inferiority; but making itself inferior to things which come into being and perish and considering itself the most contemptible and the most liable to death of all the things which it admires it could not possibly have any idea of the nature and power of God."

(*Enneads*: V, 1, i)

"Here lies the essence of all truly human evil, which consists in *breaking away from the basis of one's being*, in the *refusal of one's true origin* and in *atheistic alienation*. Plotinus' teaching is, essentially, a therapy for returning to oneself, an exhortation to engage in interior reflection so as to open up selfish closeness (the will 'to belong to oneself') and put a stop to the waste caused by unruly passions ('running the opposite course').

Selfishness is no more than a failing of the original power of love and liberality which is the essence of every spiritual being. It is a fault 'due to lack of vigour', a degradation and corruption of the deepest human energy no longer able to elevate itself, within the most intimate recess of the mind where the sense of the Sacred abides. Thus passions, instead of being mere 'alterations' of the body, become 'agitations' of the soul, deviating it, as in a dream, from its true life. They all rise from a debasement of Eros, from its becoming 'earthly' and renouncing *That* true love of man for his own *dignitas*, for the beauty of his own soul.

The way of liberation, according to Plotinus, lies in the 'purification' or our 'inner sight' (I, 6, viii) so that the soul may recognize itself in all its original decorum.[1]

1. P. Prini: *Plotino*. Abete - Roma.

11

TRANSMIGRATION

Q. People speak of reincarnation, of metempsychosis, rebirth, transmigration. What do these terms mean? And who is it that is reborn or transmigrates?

A. All the branches of Tradition have faced the problem of rebirth. The Western Mysteric Tradition speaks about metempsychosis, the Oriental—in which Buddhism, Taoism and Jainism may be included—about transmigration or rebirth.

The concept of transmigration or rebirth implies, obviously, that there is something which leaves and which comes back, something which creates movement or changes condition. Further questions may be asked: why does one transmigrate, why is one reborn? This point is very important and very much discussed. First of all let us restate the problem in metaphysical terms: that which is 'born', if it really is so, cannot be born a second time; that which is not born cannot be born or come into existence, because it is an eternal presence, an absolute or a constant. The non-existent cannot either be born or exist or be.

Therefore, if the *ātman*-constant, the pure Spirit, the Absolute in us or the pure Being cannot be born because it simply *is*, nor can it transmigrate because it is not subject to change, then what is it in us that transmigrates? And why does it transmigrate, why is it reborn?

In order to understand who is reborn and why, we must know the make-up of the manifested entity in its psycho-physical components. In this way we shall be able to examine the whole problem in all its details.

As we have already seen, according to the Western Mysteric Tradition man is a synthesis of *noûs, psyché* and *sôma*; according to the *Vedānta* Tradition he is a synthesis of *ātman, jīva* and *jīvabhūta*. The *noûs*, like the *ātman*, being the constant, the immortal, the non-born and the Absolute in us cannot, obviously, be subject to birth and transmigration. The immortal cannot become mortal, nor can the mortal become immortal, as Gauḍapāda states in his *kārikās* to the *Māṇḍūkya Upaniṣad.*

The body or bodies of the entity, being as perishable as flies, disintegrate, and their elements return to the plane and to the existential element from which they have been drawn. They cannot transmigrate or be reborn because, being compounds, they dissolve and disintegrate leaving no traces behind them.

The *jīva* or *psyché* is a reflection of consciousness of the *ātman-noûs,* it is a ray of pure consciousness which, though being a mere ray, has within itself being-will, consciousness-intelligence and creativity. It attracts towards itself a certain amount of substance from the existential planes of Being, producing its bodies of manifestation through which it can experience the various objects of the senses.

> "An eternal fragment of Me, having become in the world of mortals a living soul (*jīvabhūta*), attracts towards itself the (five) senses and the mind (*manas*) as the sixth organ, which find their basis in *prakṛti.*"
>
> (*Bhagavadgītā*: XV, 7)

If the *ātman* belongs to the state of Being—and therefore, being immortal, cannot transmigrate—, if the body belongs to the condition of non-being, and therefore has no life of its own or *aseity,* then we must shift our attention to two very important factors: the reflection-*jīva-psyché* and the qualities that represent the 'scent' of the substance.

"The vital breath" writes René Guénon in his *L'homme et son devenir selon le Vedānta,* paraphrasing a number of chapters of the *Bṛhadāraṇyaka Upaniṣad, Chāndogya Upaniṣad* and *Brahma-sūtra,* which deal with the question of death, "accompanied by all its other functions and faculties (already reabsorbed in it and not subsisting in it except as possibilities, having now reverted to the state of indifferentiation from which they had to rise in order to actually manifest themselves during life) is in turn reabsorbed by the living soul (*jīvātman,* particular manifestation of the Self at the core of human individuality, as already explained, and distinct from the Self so long as that individuality endures as such, though this distinction is an illusion from the standpoint of the absolute reality for which there is nothing but the Self); and it is this very living soul (as the reflection of the Self and central principle of the individuality) which governs the whole of the individual faculties (considered in their integrality and not only in their relationship with the corporeal mode). Like the servants of a King gather around him when he is about to undertake a journey, even so all the vital functions and faculties of the individual (external and internal) gather around the living soul (or rather within it, from which they all issue and by which they are all reabsorbed) at the last moment (of life, in the ordinary sense of the word, that is of manifested existence at the gross state), when this living soul is about to leave its corporeal form. Thus, accompanied by all its faculties (as it contains and keeps them as possibilities) it retires into a luminous individual essence (that is, into the subtle form, compared to a fiery vehicle, as we have explained with regard to *taijasa*, the second condition of *ātman*), which is composed of the five *tanmātras* or suprasensible elementary essences (just as the body has the five *bhūtas* or corporeal and sensible elements), in a subtle state (as opposed to the gross state, which is the state of external or bodily manifestation whose cycle, as far as the individual is concerned, is completed).

"As a result (due to his passage into the subtle form, described as luminous) the vital breath is said to withdraw into the Light, without meaning by this the fiery principle in the exclusive sense (as in reality it concerns an individualized reflection of the intelligible Light, a reflection the nature of which is basically the same as the mental one during bodily life and which, on the other hand, implies a combination of the five basic principles of the five elements as its support or vehicle). This withdrawal does not necessarily imply an immediate transition; in fact, (to give an example) a traveller is said to travel from a city to another, even though he may stop at one or more cities in between.

"This withdrawal from or leaving the bodily form (as described so far) is common to the ignorant person (*avidvān*) and to the contemplative Sage (*vidvān*), up to the point at which their respective (and from now on different) ways part."

Q. What are the qualities we spoke about?

A. The qualities—*sattva, rajas, tamas*—are allotropical states of *prakṛti* (substance-matter). An instinct, a desire, a passion, etc., are *prakṛtic* qualities; these qualities manifest themselves in a body-vehicle and, if coagulated, survive the body. The fragrance lives on in the air even when, for example, a flower has disappeared or the bottle of perfume has broken. A pain-pleasure caused by an event remains even when the event has vanished.

While the *sôma-sthūlaśarīra* or *jīvabhūta* supplies the instrument of pain-pleasure or of the qualities, the latter, when they survive, cling to that reflection of consciousness represented by the experiencer. Let us say that ideals, feelings, instincts, etc., can survive physical death. And as these qualities belong to the psychic dimension we can conclude that the psychic vehicle (which is not the Self) can survive the physical one.

Q. How might we express ourselves in psychological terms?

A. A crystallized psychic content can survive the dissolution of the physical compound. The *Vedānta* speaks in fact of *vāsanās*, of *saṃskāras*, that represent the 'colours', the 'odours', the tendencies, the psychic qualitative predispositions. These tendencies, stored up in our own spatiality and not dissolved, survive the death of the body.

Q. How do the *vāsanās* arise?

A. When the reflection of consciousness experiences and *adheres* to a quality it produces a *vāsanā*, or a content; the energy coagulates and becomes mass. It is obvious that in this condition the experiencer is determined by the content which, being continually nourished, grows powerful and capable of dominating the experiencer himself. The energetic power of the dream dominates the dreamer.

Q. Why do we transmigrate then?

A. We transmigrate because the unresolved qualitative mass-contents demand expression on the existential plane best suited to their maturity and relief.

Q. But is it the same individual who transmigrates?

A. That individual, with a name and a form, cannot transmigrate because he no longer subsists on the death of his vehicles. The empirical self is the outcome of the *ahaṃkāra* vehicle combination; when the vehicle disappears the *ahaṃkāra* returns to its potential state. And when both disappear there is no individuality. There is the *person* in his supraindividual state.

The qualities in themselves have no name, not has the reflection of consciousness a name. The qualities become individualized through the vehicles and the sense of ego (*ahaṃkāra*). A name is the indication of an energetic complex which has assumed individuality, which has determined itself, which has forced upon itself a circumference. We can say that in most cases individuals are simply passive *mediums* in the hands of 'entities-qualities' (*guṇas*) in search of expression or maturity.

Q. Is embodiment a school needed to advance and evolve towards the *ātman*?

A. The one Tradition has never taught the evolutionary concept. Let us examine the problem in metaphysical terms. The *ātman* or Being *is* and does not become, therefore it cannot evolve.

The qualities do not evolve but simply change aspect. Cold and heat do not evolve, just as hate and love do not. Individuality, with any name or form, does not evolve (it may undergo some adaptation) because it is the synthesis of an energetic compound which expresses itself through various qualitative aspects (*guṇas*). It is born and it dies.

Q. Is it proper to speak of reincarnation?

A. It depends on the meaning one wishes to give to the word. Let us say that the question may be posed in different terms. As we have already seen, the universe or the manifestation is composed of three vibratory states or levels which, however, represent a whole. The *jīvātman* is now on one now on another existential level. It passes through 'changes of state', of condition, and those passages—we may call them transmigrations—are caused by the *guṇas* and by the individualized and crystallized *vāsanās*.

Again, we may say that just as an individual urged by certain needs and qualities migrates, for example, from Europe to America, therefore changing his life style, so the reflection of consciousness, urged by certain qualities, transmigrates from one state to another or from one world (*loka*) to another.[1]

There is nothing dramatic or tragic in all this; it is an event that occurs automatically (in the case of the majority of beings), innocently and naturally. If the event is held to be dramatic, often tragic, it is because the entity is not aware of the process of transmigration, or else is a prisoner of a simple fear or 'change'.

Q. Therefore, it is not the 'I' of this time-space that transmigrates.

A. The empirical self is simple *phenomenon* connected with time-space. The empirical self of one particular moment is not the self of another.

In a particular time-space we can say: *I am happy*, in another time-space, following that one, we may say: *I am in conflict.* The two egos are not the same, because they annul one another in their contradiction. The empirical self is a contingent factor, an expressive moment of certain qualities (*guṇas*).

Q. Therefore it is the Soul that reincarnates or transmigrates.

A. According to the Tradition, the Soul itself is a mere reflection of the pure Spirit or *ātman*, and it is non-absolute; it dwells in a dimension (upper *taijasa*) which is not the dense physical one (*viśva*); from that dimension, as we mentioned before, it manifests itself on the lower *taijasa* plane (the *astral* plane in Western Occultism) and on the *viśva* (dense physical) plane through one of its rays of Consciousness.

Its movement (transmigration) produces expressions of qualities, causes and effects. If the empirical self—related to

1. For the various *lokas*, cp. the chapter *The Three States of Being*, in this book.

the dense physical body, to the vital body (*prāṇa*) and to the mental body—is a simple contingent factor, the *jīvātman* is relatively persistent, so as to appear eternal to the empirical ego. But the transmigration-movement of a quality occurs also within the same incarnation.

Q. How can this be possible?

A. For example, a desire *is born* (the beginning of the movement), it tends towards a particular object (path of motion) and it *dies* with its satisfaction and maturity. If we assume that the seed-germ (*vāsanā-saṃskāra*) of desire is not resolved, gradually a new desire *is born* and transmigrates towards a new object *to die* in it.

As long as the root or germ of desire exists, the quality (*guṇa*) transmigrates from one object to another, from a space to another. And obviously the ego-desire of one movement is not that of another because the empirical self, being becoming-movement, is not constant; in other words it is not Being, just as the *jīvātman* itself is not Being.

Q. Must these qualities-entities transmigrate necessarily on to the dense physical plane?

A. These crystallized qualities-entities transmigrate wherever they can express and manifest themselves, following the Law of attraction-repulsion or of syntonization. In the multiple states of Being there is room for the expression of all the possible *prakṛtic* qualities.

Q. Is there reincarnation for the Liberated?

A. If one is Liberated one can no longer transmigrate. For the Liberated all becoming-movement has ceased; he has returned to his true Homeland ('my Kingdom is not of this world'), and he does not wish to go anywhere; having no *vāsanās* nor individualized qualities to express, he has no desire, no past and no future.

Transmigration implies that something has been left unfinished, incomplete, but for him who stands *still*, like a hub of a wheel, there is no more coming or going, no birth or death because such events belong to a consciousness that has not yet grasped its own essence.

12

ANALOGY, IDENTITY AND SYMBOLOGY

Q. What can an analogy or a symbol represent?

A. "He created these worlds, the Heavenly Ocean, the shining Rays, Death, the Waters. The Heavenly Ocean is there, beyond the Heavens, and the Heavens are its foundation; the Rays are the intermediate space; Death is the earth. Below the earth are the Waters"

(*Aitareya Upaniṣad*: I, 2)

"The moon is, in fact, the door of the heavenly world."

(*Kauṣītakī Upaniṣad*: I, 2)

"The Dawn is the head of the sacrificial horse, the sun is its eye, the wind its breath, the *vaiśvānara* fire its open jaws, the year its being."

(*Bṛhadāraṇyaka Upaniṣad*: I, i, 1)

Elsewhere we read that the universe is composed of earth, air and sky, or of three states called *Virāṭ, Hiraṇyagarbha* and *Īśvara*, as well as of a fourth state called *Turīya*.

If we were to take terms such as ocean, space, sky, air or atmosphere, waters, etc., literally, we would arrive at the conclusion that these writings were fables, or that they were sibylline games for people with nothing to do, or again the myths of a primitive people devoid of common sense. And, in fact, for some people it is actually so.

But the fact is that these texts speak of a knowledge of Being and non-being, of the Infinite and of the relative, of noumenon and phenomenon, topics which do not at all belong to primitive minds but to true philosophers (here we shall not speak of the non-human inspiration of certain texts and doctrines).

In the *Bṛhadāraṇyaka Upaniṣad* (First reading) and in the *Chāndogya Upaniṣad* (VI, ii, I), for example, it is stated that

Being is the irradiation of Non-being and that from Being the determinations of phenomenal manifestation emerged. However much one would like us to believe these to be nothing but myths created by primitive minds we feel we cannot, in all honesty, support such a belief.

> "From non-being lead me to Being,
> from darkness lead me to light,
> from death lead me to immortality."
>
> (*Bṛhadāraṇyaka Upaniṣad*: I, iii, 27)

When we first approach a science—whether it be philosophy or not—in order to interpret it properly we should refer to a number of basic principles, otherwise we risk incurring serious errors of judgment.

First of all, every science has its own peculiar terminology, its own conceptual framework and reference structure which has to be kept in mind. Furthermore, the time in which the science or philosophy was drawn up has to be taken into due account. Thus, the Egyptian hieroglyphs are not pictures or drawings for children, but a particular language of the times which corresponds to precise ideas, even of a metaphysical order.

We can say that in every age and at every place the different branches of science have had their own language and their own particular 'hieroglyph'. What else is the chemical formula for water H_2O, but a kind of hieroglyph? And yet this formula contains a basic truth, encloses an idea which only the 'experts' can decipher.

What are words such as 'air', 'sky', 'golden egg', 'waters', etc., intended to represent, and what are they?

When—at the human level—we wish to show or communicate a truth that has been experienced or revealed, the only means we have available is language, which can take on different possibilities of expression: figurative, analogical, symbolic, discoursive, metaphysical, etc.

A traditional or initiatory Teaching is in most cases symbolic, sometimes figurative or analogical. Why? For two fundamental reasons: because by means of symbols, or analogies, it seeks to *evoke* within the disciple the symbolized truth, seeing that the initiatory truth is not meant for the analytical mind, but for the 'heart' of the disciple and because the symbol and the analogy reach beyond time and space. When we express ourselves by means of formulae such as: *the Sun is the living universal God,* this makes one understand that the sun as a symbol is not only valid for us and for those living at the time of the Egyptian king Amenhotep-Akhenaton, but that it is a powerful symbol veiling a metaphysical truth. The analogy between the physical sun and the metaphysical one is adequate and is in line with the traditional Science.

It is evident, however, that he who does not know the key to traditional Science may commit a serious mistake and consider the physical sun as being *identical* with God or with the supreme Being. Analogy does not mean identity, and a symbol, taken at its face value, is an empty image and devoid of meaning. The cross, for example, is a symbol which not only encloses a precise initiatory truth but which, by its very nature being synthetical, also encloses a number of different truths, depending upon the level or system of co-ordinates one may wish to relate it to. Hence the Science of the symbol, which cannot be the object of discoursive transmission: and it cannot be so for many reasons.

To say to a person that the word-symbol 'sky'—or 'waters', 'golden egg', 'ocean', etc.—, encloses a precise state of consciousness, a 'dimension' or a 'level' of Being, is of little use. Reality as such is unspeakable and can only be communicated through symbols, analogies, images, hieroglyphs. If a symbol-analogy succeeds in finding its way into the consciousness of a person, it may be able to reveal its esoterical significance.

The *Veda-Upaniṣads,* just to take one branch of the philosophical Tradition, or *Philosophia perennis,* into consideration, are of a symbolic, analogical, figurative order. Many of its terms, such as *Brahman, ātman, Īśvara, jīva, Śiva,* etc., are profoundly symbolical. They represent precise states of consciousness, 'functions', 'dimensions' or realms of Being. To consider *Brahman* to be mere physical water or the physical sun or the air, composed of oxygen and hydrogen, means being very far from the correct interpretation of the symbol.

To believe that the 'mercury' of Alchemy—another branch of the Tradition—is the mercury contained in thermometers to take the temperature means being simple-minded.

Ātman is the atomic nucleus which, although giving life and movement to its electronic sheaths, remains unaltered and equidistant. This is an analogy, an image, but not an identity. There is an abyss between the physical atom and the *ātman*.

The term 'symbol' comes from the Greek word *symbolon* and indicates two halves or corresponding parts of an object kept by two different persons as a sign of recognition. *Symbolon* also means 'divine sign', 'password', 'mark of distinction', etc. This suggests the idea that when the two halves are joined together again and match, unity, that is synthesis, is attained once more. When the celestial Ocean and the Earth are reunited, they recognize each other as unity—and the Harmony of the spheres resounds in Space-life.

The contrary of *symbolon* is *diabolos* which means: to throw across, to calumniate to oppose, to contrast, to distort, to deceive; in other words, to divide. And that which divides or separates is *ahaṃkāra* or the sense of ego, and *manas* or the empirical mind.

13

KARMA OR THE LAW OF CAUSE AND EFFECT

Q. People speak of *karma*, sin, law of retaliation, reparation, etc. What do these words mean?

A. We have to distinguish what is a philosophical vision of Reality from a sentimental-anthropomorphous or religio-theistic one.

The theistic, anthropomorphous outlook brings God or Being down to the 'human dimension', endowing it with qualities of love-hate or of attraction-repulsion. God is infinite goodness but He is also the punisher of those who go against His will. Down through the ages many religions have drawn inspiration from this dual God, even if they spoke of 'One God'.

The relationship of man-God based upon these assumptions leads to a stressing of the moral aspect because, depending on his conduct, man may conform to or trespass the will of God. Sin is a psychological attitude which infringes or violates the law of God. Since moral behaviour implies a set of norms to conform to, the anthropomorphous theistic religion has a code, considered to be divine, which each believer must obey. Disobedience is followed by sin; those who do not obey or conform to the law sin. Hence the 'reparation' which is necessary in order to be permitted back into the 'grace' of the offended God. As religious theism attributes to God alone the principle of will, man is left with just the choice to obey or disobey; yet, although he may obey, the verdict of absolution remains exclusively in the hands of God. God is the arbiter of the entire destiny of mankind, introducing Himself into human affairs in time and space. He may concede or refuse his forgiveness, according to His inscrutable designs.

The *nèmesis* of the Sacred Mysteries is the equivalent of the

Vedic *karma*. The word *karma* means ritual action, but also law of cause and effect. What is this law?

On the psycho-spiritual level, just as on the physical level, every effect is the materialization of a cause. We might say that the law of *karma* is similar to that of cause-and-effect of science.

Man has the possibility to move in several directions, producing effects which may or may not be in harmony with himself and with others. *Nèmesis* consists in re-establishing Order and equilibrium where unbalance and disorder have occurred. By upsetting the balance or creating disharmony in the universal Order the *mystēs* receives a repercussion. It is the law of *nèmesis* that comes in and operates so that the Order is re-established.

If we put a finger into the fire (cause) the effect will be a burn. However, this does not imply that a vindictive or emotional God has punished us and applied the law of retaliation. Our ignorance (*avidyā*) of a law has led us into *error*.

A powerful energy of hatred or love attracts towards itself energy of the same nature and strength. The effect is proportionate to the cause. There is nothing extraordinary in the fact that a discharge, let us say, of hate attracts hate. It is the law of magnetic sympathy in action.

When Jesus said to love those who hate us, he did not wish to announce a principle of social and sentimental morality. Rather, he wished to point out a universal law. If hate attracts hate, then in order to neutralize a force of a certain nature and intensity it is necessary to use another of equal and opposite strength. The law of the Initiate is: love your enemy.

Ignorance is won over by knowledge, inertia by determination, pessimism by optimism, and hate by love.

The law of *karma-nèmesis* has been laid down by the Sacred Science.

In order to understand certain things properly one has to consider that a dense physical form is a complex of energy with qualities and a producer of causes and effects and that the individual is a center of consciousness around which qualified energies generating causes and effects revolve. Just as studying physics allows us to know how the mechanism of the law of cause and effect works, so studying the Sacred Science allows us to understand the manner in which the law of *karma* operates.

We must recognize the fact that many events, even negative ones, to which we are subjected, are not produced by God but by ourselves, because we are the ones who set the law of *karma* in motion. But if we wish to neutralize an energy, we obviously need another powerful energy to contrast it. This is where many fail, as they believe they do not possess sufficient energy capable of producing a contrary cause.

In order to overcome the earth gravity force, man has had to use not only a force equal and opposite to it, but also an amount of extra energy by which to transcend it altogether. The universe, at all levels, is governed by laws (*dharma*) and a correct understanding of the law can give the individual the possibility not only to *harmonize* with nature but also—and this is a consequence—to positively affect and harmonize what we call his own destiny.

The sorrow-conflict of the world of men is not brought about by a capricious and emotional God, but by man himself who has not yet understood the operative dynamics of some of the laws governing the universe and the individual.

Man can use, manipulate and direct forces, energies and therefore, he alone is responsible for the effects these actions imply.

The *Vedānta*, with reference to the individual, names three kinds of *karma: āgāmin, saṃcita* and *prārabdha*. Śaṃkara, in his *Vivekacūḍāmaṇi* (verse 453), says: "The *prārabdhakarma* is too powerful for the realized being to stop; it will exhaust with the extinction of its fruit. The other two kinds of *karma*, that resulting from previous actions (*saṃcita*) and that whose effects are not mature (*āgāmin*), will be burnt to ashes by the fire of knowledge. However, none of these three kinds of *karma* is capable of affecting the ascetic who has realized *Brahman* and lives in identity with It."

Prārabdhakarma is the matured kind of *karma* and is therefore the current one: having taken on a physical body is a *prārabdhakarma* because it is a matured one. The physical body is here and we cannot destroy it. To have a child is also a *prārabdhakarma* because a child, once it has been brought into being, cannot be sent back.

The other two kinds of *karma*, not having come into objective existence, can be stopped and even extinguished or resolved because the favouring causes have been removed. The cause of the *karmic* causes is *avidyā*, the metaphysical ignorance which concerns the nature of Being; when it is resolved the *karma* vanishes and even the *prārabdha*, for the *jñāni-asparśin*, is as if it did not exist because it has no grasp upon his freed consciousness.

> "The *brāhmaṇa*, having recognized that the different worlds are the outcome of the accumulated *karma*, feels disgusted with them because by means of what is created one cannot realize the Non-created. . . ."
>
> (*Muṇḍaka Upaniṣad*: I, ii, 12)

14

THE SIDDHIS

Q. When one speaks of *yoga*, or of Oriental teachings, the so-called 'powers' or *siddhis* come immediately to one's mind. But what are these powers?

A. Much confusion and misunderstanding can arise with regard to this particular topic. Quite apart from the correct attitude of consciousness that is required towards the different kinds of *yoga* or traditional Doctrines, we have to recognize the fact that many conceive of Realization as the achievement or acquisition of the so-called 'powers'.

First of all, we must make some distinctions. In psychological terms, a power is a *faculty* or an *ability* inherent in matter itself, and it may be considered as a quality or attribute of it. In philosophical terms 'power' means 'possibility': the possibility of a being to perform or express an act.

We should make a further distinction between what is called a 'psychic power' and a psychological faculty; the latter bears reference more specifically to the mind in general. The mental perception, that everyone has, is a psychological faculty which concerns the *psyché* and not the *sôma* aspect.

The psychic power as such represents the development of particular 'senses' or sensory organs which grants the ability to 'hear' and 'see' upon planes that go beyond the dense physical one. As at the physical level we have the senses which bring us into contact with the gross-material plane, so too at the subtle, supraphysical level we have other senses which connect us with that existential level or plane.

Besides physical, we have psychic seeing (clairvoyance), and hearing (clairaudience) by which we perceive subtle objects and sounds which escape the ordinary range of physical perception. We can say that a psychic power is a faculty of the 'psyche' existing as a reality apart from the physical body-*sôma*.

The majority seek psychic powers for two reasons:

(1) because, being a simple extension of the empirical self upon the subtle psychic plane, the self is not hampered by them, rather it is magnified and strengthened. The majority are after the expansion of their ego, not its solution and transcendence.

(2) because they represent a compensation for the weakness, failings and limitations of individuality.

Similarly, at the physical level many are after wealth, which is a material 'power', in order to feel stronger, more confident and ego-centered. Not having found security and peace of mind within themselves they compensate this failing through wealth. In fact we know that wealth becomes an all-important compensation for those who *are not.* Even intellectual 'power' may be a compensation. The wealth given by the psychic power meets this need, it compensates for many a deficiency of the empirical self because, in truth, the ego *is not.*

However, if psychic powers belong to the self, and the worldly or empirical self is marked by uncompleteness, by lacking and by relativity, then the powers inherent in it belong to the realm of *avidyā,* to use *Vedāntic* terminology.

An entity may be clairvoyant, clairaudient, levitating, telepathic, psychometric, etc., but this is of little importance because such a person belongs to and moves within the sphere of *avidyā.*

Those who are after the psychic power for its own sake may represent interesting subjects for psychoanalysis. At times these persons waste an entire existence in order to become mediocre clairvoyants, extra-sensorially perceptive 'mediums', etc.

With reference to psychic powers there is a very revealing anecdote concerning the Buddha. As the story goes, one day, upon entering a woody place, the Buddha met a meditating 'santon'. On seeing the Buddha, he went out to meet him and asked him to express his opinion about the ascesis he had carried on for so many years.

A large river was nearby and the 'santon', lifting himself up into the air, crossed over the waters. When he came back before the Buddha he urged him to pronounce himself. The Buddha, not in the least ruffled, asked: "How long has it taken you to acquire the power of levitating?" The 'santon' replied: 'Twenty years'. And the Buddha said: "With five rupees I can cross this river in a boat in as few as five minutes."

The 'power' is not Realization of the *ātman* because, being a *faculty*, it belongs to *prakṛti*. 'Powers' operate within the sphere of duality; they imply three factors: an entity holding a power, the power, and an object to which the power is applied. The power, by operating in the dual and multiple world, cannot be the fount of *ānanda*, cannot be the source of *Completeness-Pax profunda* which is connatural to Being.

The greatest power that can be attained is that of Illumination, or the *satori*, the *Parā Vidyā*, the gnosis and this power does not belong any longer to the psychic realm but to the strictly spiritual one. In this sphere the individual, with all his toy-powers, no longer exists because he is completely transcended.

Q. However, we know of true Saints who use powers.

A. They are Saints not because they use powers but because they are Illuminated. If occasionally they use some psychic faculties, it is to make an emotional impression upon the masses—which in fact need such things—rather than to indicate the pathway of Illumination.

A Saint may make use of powers as a momentary means by which to draw the attention of the unbeliever, while mere individuality needs power as psychological compensation.

Q. You said before that a power is a faculty which influence the environment. What difference is there between this influence and that of the Saint?

A. The difference is great indeed. The influence of a power acts:

(1) upon the psycho-physical (individualized) plane;
(2) upon the plane of force-energy;
(3) within the field of subject-object duality;
(4) upon the plane of the ego's will;
(5) in order to obtain a physical or psychological advantage.

The influence of the Realized one operates:

(1) upon the spiritual (universal) plane;

(2) upon the plane of 'innocence', of non-resistance. The influence of the Realized one is irradiation that expands naturally, like the fragrance of a flower;

(3) within the field of pure Subject, because it does not pay any attention to the object. The Realized one does not try or seek or desire to influence others.

(4) Upon the plane of non-will, non-desire, because it has no selfish aims;

(5) therefore, upon the plane of 'donation', of pure Love, since it is his own particular consciousness vibration that resounds.

Thus, while psychic powers operate in the sphere of individualized existence, spiritual power acts within the sphere of the supraindividual or the universal.

The influence of the Realized one becomes a 'magnetic field' at the centre of the world, while that of the psyche is a simple relationship between a single subject and an object.

Q. Can we say, therefore, that the Realized one 'vibrates' *sat-cit-ānanda*, while the person who has psychic powers must use a force, a faculty in order to obtain certain effects?

A. Yes, indeed. The Realized one is pure Consciousness without superimposition, he is Being, while the person having psychic powers is an individuality speaking to other individualities by means of tools of 'persuasion'.

Q. Can power be used simply out of vanity?

A. Yes. This is the less harmful of possibilities, even if the most fleeting. Vanity is one of the many psychological 'advantages' that one may receive from the exercise of a power.

Q. Are power-faculties mere accidents of *prakṛti* after all?

A. Yes. Instead *sat, cit, ānanda* are not attributes or accidents of Being, but are *nature* of Being. They are consubstantial with Being itself.

Bliss-fulfilment is not a psychic power; Intelligence or Consciousness is not a psychic power. A psychic power is the faculty to perceive sensorially, behind which operate the Universal Intelligence, Being and Consciousness.

Power represents the exercise of a faculty which can come into being and die, can exist or cannot exist. It operates, as we have already said, upon the plane of duality, therefore on the plane of non-being. *Sat-cit-ānanda* is Being, it is ever-existent since it belongs to non-becoming.

Power operates upon the plane of necessity, while *sat-cit-ānanda* acts upon the plane of *freedom*.

Material or psychic wealth is needed to acquire something that one does not possess; he who possesses everything within himself does not seek either material or psychic wealth.

Q. Does the metaphysical pathway oppose such powers?

A. It cannot oppose them, as they are powers and faculties that belong to *prakṛti* itself. It cannot, obviously, agree with the use that is often made of them. Even Jesus made use of similar powers and these were not only used with understanding but we can say that they did not belong to the psychic sphere as this sphere represented just a channel of the universal Will. The universal Consciousness was making use of 'phenomena' for certain, and obviously non-individual, purposes.

INDEX